LET ME LOVE YOU DARLING

Marie L. Pennington

Contents

Prologue

"Violet, I need new school shoes, " wailed nine year old Walter Nelson looking at his old school shoes which seriously needed replacement as he had outgrown them. His twin, William, looked at his own shoes too but didn't utter a word to their nineteen year old sister Violet. He could see that she was struggling to make ends meet.

Violet sighed as she saw their school shoes. She knew they needed a new pair but she didn't have any money. A week more to go till she received her pay. There were bills to pay and food to be put on the table. Still she would buy their shoes first after getting her salary.

"Just give me a week, Walt," she pleaded and they nodded, disappearing to their room.

Violet Nelson couldn't attend college last year after graduating from high school when her mom died. Her mom, Maria Nelson had separated from her drunkard husband, Jimmy Nelson seven years back.

Maria Nelson had brought the children, Violet, and her two brothers with her to W Crest Boulevard in south LA. It was her parents house in a cheap affordable complex when they were alive. She worked at a local departmental store as a manager and they led a good life. After her death in a car accident, Violet and her siblings at least had a roof over their heads to call their own. It was a small two bedroomed apartment with a tiny living area with a kitchen fitted into one corner and it was home to the Nelson family.

Their neighbour, Mary Jane Lee was a sweet woman thirty years older than her who lived with her husband, Michael Lee and 10 year old son Emmett. She worked as the restaurant manager at a five star hotel, Parker Suites in Beverly Hills, LA.

After her mom's death, she helped Violet get a job in her hotel. Due to her lack of qualifications, all she got was the job of a housekeeping staff. Still the pay was good and Violet had no other alternative than to continue. Mary Jane gave her a lift to the hotel in the mornings and in the evenings after duty she took the hotel's shuttle bus till Galveston street and then walked home.

After changing she went to work as a waitress for four hours at a small cafe near Galveston street and returned home late by 9 o'clock. The extra pay helped her a lot as she had to spend on her brothers' education too. She couldn't afford to take any day off.

It was a Saturday and she had to get ready for work. Emmett came in with his old books and went to the boys room to dump them. She didn't have money to buy so many books and Emmett's older ones helped the twins a lot.

While she and Mary Jane went to work, Michael stayed at home and looked after the three boys. He worked at the departmental store at the cash counter and had two days off, Saturday and Sunday. It helped them as they could go to work without having to bother about the kids.

She quickly got ready wearing a white shirt and a pair of denims. She fixed her chestnut brown hair into a tight bun and packed her uniform in a carry bag. She picked up her handbag and rushed out.

"Walt, Will, be good and listen to uncle Mike. I'll see you tonight, " she yelled on her way out.

"Don't worry, we will. Bye," they chorused and she left with a smile on her face.

She went next door and was just about to ring the doorbell when it flung open and Mary Jane rushed out wearing a pair of black trousers and a pale pink top.

"We're late, let's hurry. Hope the traffic's not a bother today," she said with a laugh and they climbed down the narrow stairs to the ground floor. Her Ford Focus was parked below and they climbed onto it and sped off. They had to start at 6:30 in the morning to beat the traffic.

"I'll speak to Dominic for a raise of your pay. That way you can leave that waitress job, Violet. I seriously don't like it," she said frankly.

Dominic Evans was the HR manager at Parker Suites and kept all the employees in a very tight line.

"Thanks Mary. I'd really appreciate that but he won't listen," Violet told her. She knew it. Last month Dominic made her clean the penthouse upstairs, everyday where the owner of Parker Suites, the sinfully gorgeous Lucas Parker stayed whenever he was in LA. Dominic hadn't even considered giving her a raise for the extra cleaning and she didn't ask. She just did her duty, cleaning her employer's apartment to the best of her abilities. Thankfully, he was always away when she went upstairs to clean which made her work all the more easier for her.

They reached Beverly Hills in an hour's time and parking the car in the employees parking spaces, they went inside. While Mary Jane went to talk to Dominic, she went to change into her uniform.

Inside the washroom, she heard her colleagues, Greta and Cassidy talking, "He's a player. I heard that he slept with his brother's wife and caused a divorce between them," said Greta, the gossip queen.

She knew they were talking about Lucas Parker and his million affairs. True, he was the hottest topic at Parker Suites but she really didn't have any time to indulge in such gossip.

"Really? I know he's notorious but he's so droolworthy, I'd jump into bed anytime if I could," said Cassidy, with dreamy eyes.

"Hey girl, you're engaged," said Greta, frowning at her. "Leave Lucas for us single girls. What say Violet?" Said Greta.

"You're welcome to him, Greta. I have to provide for my brother's, I can't afford it," Violet said, quickly changing into her uniform which was a black pencil skirt and a white shirt with black pipings around the half sleeves and collar. The hotel's name was embroidered onto the chest. She pulled her hair into a neat bun and pinned her name badge onto her chest above the hotel's name.

"If I had your looks, believe me, I would," said Greta who was seven years older than her.

Violet smiled,"With your own good looks you can. All the best," Violet said with a smile and left the washroom. She had a huge workload and she had no time to stand and chat.

She went to the house keeping room and got her trolley with the cleaning stuff. Dominic came out of his office with the housekeeping Head, Sarah Browning.

"Violet, you have to go to the penthouse now and clean it," said Sarah, looking at Violet with a smile. She was a very nice middle aged woman who looked too strict to those who didn't perform but she liked Violet. Violet was as old as her own daughter and she worked so hard that Sarah felt bad for the teenaged girl who should have been in college.

"Yes ma'am. But what about the guest suites, especially suite 101. Mr Marshall would get upset," she said, looking at them with worry. Tim Marshall was their regular customer who visited the Parker Suites regularly to hold business conferences. He was very particular about cleanliness and Violet cleaned his suite first every morning to keep him satisfied.

"I'll send Cassidy there today," said Sarah and Violet nodded. "Now go immediately."

Violet didn't understand what the urgency was today. She went to clean the penthouse everyday at 11 o'clock when it's owner was away. He returned at lunchtime everyday and she would have completed by then.

She rushed into the private elevator that took her straight up to the penthouse. The elevator opened and she pushed her cleaning station towards the door of the penthouse. She punched in the code and went inside, pulling the trolley station with her. She locked the door and went to clean the kitchen first. Then she would clean the ensuites and then the bedrooms and the other rooms and lastly the living room and the reception room.

She set about her work switching on her mobile in her skirt pocket to her favourite love song and plugged the earphones into her ears.

Chapter 1

Chapter One

Lucas Parker restlessly fidgeted around in his bedroom. For a month, he had been coming to a scrupulously clean penthouse with the intoxicating smell of violets. It was a soft sweet, powdery and romantic smell which always relieved him of his stress and headaches the moment he stepped into his penthouse. He was very thankful to the employee who worked so hard to clean his huge penthouse everyday. He wanted to meet her and thank her personally and give her some money as a token of his appreciation.

He didn't go out on Saturday and summoned Dominic and Sarah early in the morning at 7 o'clock to his penthouse. They came hurrying, tensed at being called so early.

"Mrs Browning, who cleans this place, everyday," he asked Sarah.

"Sir one of our new employees does it. I will replace her if you're not satisfied," she said, nervously.

"No, please don't. In fact, I wanted to personally meet her and thank her and maybe give her some money, for her children, " Lucas said, and Sarah grinned at Dominic.

"What happened? Have I said anything wrong?" Lucas asked as Sarah and Dominic looked at each other clearly communicating in their sign language.

"Sir, I would suggest you look at her employee profile and then decide what you want to give her," said Dominic with a chuckle. Sarah went down to the HR office to get Violet's employee register.

"I hope cupid strikes him and he falls head over heels in love with this girl. Her life will improve, " said Sarah to herself as she looked at the beautiful innocent photograph of Violet in the register.

She took it upstairs and handed Violet's profile sheet to Lucas. "Is there anything else you want sir?" She asked Lucas.

"Yes, send her upstairs the moment she comes in. She could clean as well as meet me," he said and they both nodded and left.

Lucas sat down on his sofa and looked at the profile sheet Sarah gave him. The photograph of a young teenage girl with big beautiful hazel eyes staring back at him made his breath hitch. Who was this angel? He had expected some middle aged woman but not this stunning beauty. He gazed at her flawless face, her chestnut brown hair with astonishment.

Violet Nelson, he read her name. What a coincidence! She smelled of violets and her name was Violet as well. He murmured her name ten times, loving the feel of it on his tongue.

He now became desperate to meet her in person. She should be in college. Why was she working as a housekeeping staff? She might be needy, he concluded. He read her profile. She lived in south LA? That was too far away, he thought. This was her first job. She only had graduated high school and was nineteen years of age. Lucas couldn't look away from her profile sheet. He eagerly waited to meet her.

At twenty-six, he co-owned Parker Suites spanning all over the world with his cousin Tyler Parker. Their dads were brothers who started the Parker Suites together, around forty years back.

So while his dad, Eric Parker still actively managed the Parker Suites, Tyler's dad, Ethan Parker already retired and Tyler actively took over from him. Lucas's younger sister Serenity who was two years younger than him looked after the interior designing and decorations of the Parker Suites all over the world. With a degree in interior decoration and design, she was very good at her job. His youngest brother, Liam was in his third year studying hotel management while working as an intern at one of the Parker Suites in Las Vegas.

His whole family lived in Las Vegas while he spent his maximum time between LA, Washington and New York.

He had a notorious reputation thanks to his cousin Tyler's first wife, Meredith who was a bitch. She had trapped Tyler into a forced marriage for money and other gains. When Tyler realised he immediately divorced her. She tried to seduce Lucas but he didn't give her any attention. Frustrated, she lied to Tyler and tried to malign Lucas's name. She created misunderstandings between him and Tyler. Lucas didn't care. He would clear his misunderstandings with Tyler, when they met.

He went to his bedroom to take a quick shower before Violet arrived. When he came out of his ensuite, he could distinctly smell the sweet intoxicating smell of violets again. Yes she was here, in his penthouse. But where? He wore a pair of sweatpants and while drying his hair with the towel hanging from his shoulders, he went out of his bedroom in search of her.

He went to the living room, she wasn't there. He went to the kitchen, she wasn't there too, he went to the bedroom next to his, she wasn't there but he could smell her presence. He went to check the ensuite when he heard a sweet voice singing, "A thousand years" by Christina Perry. His feet stopped as he stood transfixed to the spot, listening with bated breath.

It was the most angelic voice he'd ever heard, like sweet music to his ears. She sang with so much feeling into the song. Did she love someone? He wondered, feeling a pang of jealousy already. Did she have a boyfriend? He had to find out. She sang

Heart beats fastColors and promisesHow to be braveHow can I love when I'm afraid to fallBut watching you stand aloneAll of my doubt, suddenly goes away somehow

One step closer

I have died everyday, waiting for youDarling, don't be afraid, I have loved you for a thousand yearsI'll love you for a thousand more

He couldn't take it anymore. He craved for one glimpse of her. Going towards the ensuite he stood in front of the closed door. Suddenly it opened and Violet came out and collided with his bare chest.

As she looked up at him, he was lost into those mesmerising hazel eyes. She was more breathtaking from so near. She was irresistible actually. His arms went round her soft body, loving the feel of her against his body. The sweet smell.of violets created havoc with his sense and he was lost in her.

Suddenly she looked down and extricated herself from his hold as realisation struck. Violet was too scared to have collided with Lucas Parker himself. She didn't know he was at home. She had no idea that he was so handsome and drool worthy just like Greta had said. She was shamelessly lost in his embrace. She had goosebumps the moment she touched his bare muscular chest. His embrace invoked a strange feeling inside her. A strange yearning and she was scared of falling for the casanova himself. He was way beyond her league and she was just a cleaner at one of his many hotels.

Would he report her? She looked at her feet trembling with fear.

"I'm s s sorry, sir. I didn't know you were here. I think I'll come later when it's convenient for you," she stammered and picked up her things and ran out before Lucas could come out of his trance.

Chapter 2

Chapter Two

C oming out of his trance, Lucas rushed towards the main door, but she was already gone. "Damn," he swore. Was she scared of him? She ran away without finishing her cleaning. He pondered over whether to call Sarah and summon Violet again. Then he decided to just leave it and take it easy. He would go down and seek her out after her nerves calmed down.

But what about his nerves? They were anything but calm. Why was his heart beating so fast? Was he already in love with her? How was that possible? He just had a single encounter with her.

Violet raced to Sarah's office with her heart hammering in her chest. She knocked and entered,"Ma'am, please, I'm sorry. I don't want to lose this job. I need it," she said, standing in front of Sarah as a few tear drops fell from her eyes.

"What's up Violet? Didn't you complete your work in the penthouse?" She asked trying to grasp what she was saying.

"I didn't know Mr Parker's was there. I was cleaning and accidentally bumped into him. I may have inconvenienced him. I'm sorry," she said, in a panicked tone.

Sarah smiled inwardly. So Lucas met her after all. "Did he threaten you?" She asked the scared girl.

"No, he didn't say anything, " Violet said.

"Then what did he do?" Asked Sarah with interest.

"He just, I mean, nothing," Violet stammered as her cheeks flushed red.

Sarah chuckled,"Interesting," she mumbled and Violet coloured more. "Don't worry, I'll have a word with him."

"Thank you, ma'am, " said Violet and left the room.

She got busy after that cleaning the rest of the suites. It was lunch time and since she didn't have any money to buy anything for herself, she went to the housekeeping room to drink water to fill her rumbling tummy.

"You didn't complete cleaning my penthouse today?" Said a husky male voice from just behind her. His hot breath fanning on her neck as she stood with her bottle of water.

She whirled around and came nose to nose with Lucas Parker himself. Her eyes opened wide as she gaped at him and opened and closed her mouth like a goldfish. No words came out and she was dumbstruck.

He took the bottle from her hands and placed it down. Violet came to her senses and lowered her eyes to her feet. She stepped backwards from him, putting enough distance between themselves. "I'm sorry, sir. I'll do it just now," she said, going to get a cleaning station.

"You can finish your lunch first," he told her, his eyes not leaving her face. He could see that she was tired already. His heart ached for her. She needed a break from so much work.

"It's ok. I'll clean first," she said, hurrying out of the housekeeping room to the elevators. She went inside and was about to press the button when Lucas came into the elevator with her.

"I actually wanted to thank you for cleaning my apartment so well everyday," he started and she just nodded. He wanted to say so much more but she just didn't reciprocate. He wanted to give her some gifts as a token of his appreciation but knew that she wouldn't accept them.

"It's my job, sir," she said, still looking at her feet. Lucas felt frustrated. He wanted to drown in her hazel eyes, yet she wouldn't look up at him. Other women would have been ready to jump into bed with him and here she was, scared and running away from him. It made his heart beat more fiercely for her. Why couldn't she see that he was interested in her?

They went up to his penthouse and she immediately set off to his bedroom to clean and he followed her there. Violet was confused why he was following her around. Maybe he wanted to check her work. She set about cleaning his bed first as he stood at the door leaning against it and watching her. Feeling oddly disturbed at his scrutiny, she somehow managed to change the sheets and pillow cases. She arranged the cushions and dusted the furniture as he watched her. Didn't he have any work today?

She sprayed the floral room freshener and was about to go to his en-suite when suddenly she felt him behind her. "What did you spray?" He asked coming up behind her as his arm went around her and took the air freshener from her hand.

"Air freshener, sir. I love violets, so I chose this for your apartment. I can change to roses or any other fragrance, " she said hurriedly. Her arm erupted into goosebumps where his arm brushed hers to get the room freshener.

"I love Violet," he said, his piercing eyes staring at her, holding her gaze. She blushed but couldn't look away from his blue magnetic eyes. She noticed that he didn't mention " violets" and felt more embarrassed. Was he flirting with her? She was unsure having never experienced such things in her life. She went to an all girls school and never went to college.

"I think I should complete the work, " she said, looking down at her feet and moving towards the ensuite.

"I think I want to have lunch now. Please could you warm the food? It's in the kitchen," he said and she nodded her head and walked out of the room, glad to escape him. But he still followed her to the kitchen. Lucas had become a lost puppy around her. Did love at first sight truly happen? It happened to him and was confused.

She washed her hands and warmed the food in the microwave. Lucas came up behind her. "I want you to have lunch with me, " he stated.

"No, thank you sir. You enjoy your lunch. I'll complete my cleaning, " she said, serving him on a plate.

"I'm your employer. Shouldn't you listen to me?" He asked, feeling frustrated that she was so stubborn.

She looked up at him to see if he was serious. Why was he sharing his lunch with her? The food looked delicious and she was ravenous after working so hard since morning. It was just a simple lunch invitation, no harm in that?

"Don't worry I won't eat you up unless you want me to," he said, getting a plate from the cabinet above her head. His arm brushed her cheek and she trembled at the electric jolt that ran down her body at his touch.

She blushed at his implications. "Here, your food is served sir," she said, handing him his plate.

He kept the empty plate down and took his food from her hands. "Now serve yourself or else I'll punish you," he said, looking at her.

She smiled and it made her look so young and gorgeous. "You should smile more Violet, " he said and she smiled more as she served herself too.

He led her to the dining table and they ate in silence. She could feel his hot gaze upon her as he ate his food. "So, tell me about yourself Violet, " he asked her, not removing his gaze from her.

"There's nothing to tell. I'm boring, " she informed him, enjoying her food. It was the best meal of her life.

"Let me decide that. You sing beautifully. Were you singing for your boyfriend or for someone else you love?" He asked curiously.

"You heard? Oh no, I don't have a boyfriend and neither do I love anyone. It's just my favourite song," she informed with a laugh.

"I'm glad," Lucas couldn't help but comment.

Violet coloured at his comment but continued to eat.

"So why don't you go to college?" He asked.

"I would have if my mom was alive. She died last year and I have two younger brothers to take care of," she replied.

"Oh, I'm sorry. I didn't know," he said, feeling bad for her. The more he came to know her the more he fell in love with her.

They finished eating and Violet cleaned up everything. "I need to finish my cleaning. Thank you for the lunch, sir," she said.

"Lucas," he prompted.

"What sir?" She asked, not knowing whether she heard correctly.

"Call me Lucas. And be here tomorrow at 8 in the morning, else you will be punished," he said and she nodded. Lucas left the penthouse with a smile on his lips.

He would meet her again tomorrow. In a month, he would completely make her fall in love with him just like he had fallen for her.

Chapter 3

Chapter Three

Violet completed her cleaning and left the penthouse. The whole day she only thought about Lucas. She couldn't figure out why he was being so nice to a poor employee like herself. She couldn't understand how to reciprocate to his behaviour. She was confused by her body's response towards him.

She had never been in such a dilemma before, whether to fear Lucas or respond to him. Maybe he was just showing his appreciation towards her. But why? Employees didn't at all care who cleaned their homes in their absence. Then why did Lucas care so much?

Even Sarah and Dominic noticed her restlessness and her lack of concentration in her work. She was their most dedicated staff and such an occurrence was most uncommon. Her mind was elsewhere as she kept on cleaning the same place for minutes.

"Violet, you can go home and rest. You already have finished your work," said Sarah when her time was up and yet she wasn't aware of it.

"Yes ma'am," said Violet going to the housekeeping room to keep.her stuff and change for going home. She looked at the clock and gasped. She was already twenty minutes late and had missed her shuttle bus! Now how would she go home? Mary Jane had left an hour ago.

She didn't have much money to take the metro bus or train. If she walked she would reach the late at night and then what about her cafe duty? She quickly changed and hurried outside the hotel and collided again with Lucas Parker as he was entering Parker Suites.

His arm supported her to stop her from falling over. "I'm sorry sir, I didn't see you," she said and Lucas quirked his eyebrows at her. Was the girl for real? She didn't see him? He, the most gorgeous male on the planet?

"Done for the day?" He asked, looking down at her as she gained her balance and nervously backed away.

"Yes," she said not looking up at him.

"So how do you go home?" He asked her, still staring at her. He loved the tight pair of denims which clung to her hips and legs. The soft white short shirt too clung to her, exposing her curvy figure to his eyes.

"I take the shuttle," she said, looking at the place opposite the road where the shuttle usually waited. But as luck would have it, the bus had left twenty minutes back.

"But it's gone. Now?" He asked in concern.

"I'll walk," she said with a small smile and turned to go. Walk? Seriously? Lucas was shocked to see that she seriously was thinking of walking down home.

"Violet, I will drop you, home. Come," he said, holding her arm and leading her towards his car.

"No no sir. Please don't bother. I'm used to walking," she tried to convince him. It was her problem and he was her employer and that too such a busy man. She really couldn't imagine in her wildest dreams that she would take advantage of his generosity.

"I insist," he said in earnest but she vigorously shook her head and tried to break free from his hold. "You leave me no choice," he said, suddenly picking her up bridal style and carrying her to his car.

"Sir, please put me down. Everyone's watching, " she reminded him in panic. Her eyes going to the hotel windows, scanning the entire building in a quick glance. What would everyone say when she met them tomorrow? She blushed furiously as he turned a deaf ear to her and placed her on his passenger seat. Violet loved the expensive plush insides of his beautiful sleek dark grey Jaguar XF. It smelled like him too, minty and wood combined with a masculine scent of his. She never sat inside such a luxury car in her entire nineteen years of life.

He went around and got into the driver's seat. He turned and leaned towards her. His face came closer to her, inches away from hers as he stared at her wide hazel eyes watching him with confusion. His arm went around her as he pulled her seat belt and fixed it. He couldn't look away, feeling hypnotised by those innocent green eyes.

He looked down to her kissable, moist, baby pink lips. He felt this dangerous pull towards her but he had to take it slow. He had a notorious reputation and she was very innocent and vulnerable. "Tell me your address," he asked her, still looking at her lips. There was no harm in looking. They seemed to pull him towards their plump fullness, inviting him to taste their sweetness.

Violet turned red as a tomato at his closeness. She could feel his hot gaze upon her lips and she felt too embarrassed to utter a word. "Sir, I I don't think this is a good idea," she said. Her heart was hammering in her chest and she didn't know what she would do if he kissed her. In fact, she secretly wanted him to kiss her. She'd never been kissed by any man before and from what Greta said, it was a magical thing to be thoroughly kissed.

Lucas sighed and sat straight, driving away towards south LA. "Oh, it's the best idea. Now tell me your address," he prodded.

She gave him her address and he fed it into his navigation system. "I'm going to south LA after years. I hardly have work that side with all our hotels around Beverly Hills, Marina beach and Long beach," he informed her and she smiled.

"I know else I would have searched for something closer home, " she told him. She didn't want to bother Mary Jane every morning but she had no choice actually. Although Mary Jane never complained or showed any disapproval, yet Violet felt guilty for taking advantage of her kind soul.

Lucas glanced at her with a thoughtful expression on his face for a brief second before returning his attention back to the road. He talked about his last visit to south LA with a childhood friend of his who's parents lived there. "I helped him shift them to New York," he finished with a happy smile on his face.

She stared at him, loving the genuine smile that lit up his face. He wasn't what everyone portrayed him to be. He was much more. His heart was genuinely good. He had a kind nature which he exhibited only to a selected few. And she was lucky to be one of those selective few. Although he was a billionaire, his down to earth, humble nature made her feel attracted towards him.

"Like what you see?" He asked, feeling acutely aware of her gaze upon him. He winced at his cliche pickup line, but what the hell! It was so appropriate.

She looked away immediately, as if scorched, blushing furiously at being caught checking him out. "I I wasn't looking, " she stammered.

He grinned, "Sure, I'm transparent maybe," he said, winking at her. She blushed more and looked out of the window.

"The left turn ahead and we'll reach," she guided him.

He turned towards her street as everyone stared at the luxurious car that entered the neighbourhood. He stopped in front of her building. "Thank you sir," she said, getting down.

"I'm coming up for coffee," he stated, locking his car and following her up the stairs.

Chapter 4

Chapter Four

Lucas saw the neighbourhood and immediately understood how much she needed her job. The stairs were too steep and chipped off from the edges. They were badly in need of repairing but in an affordable housing complex no one had the funds to repair it. He simply followed her wordlessly up the stairs.

Violet chewed her lips nervously as she climbed up the stairs. She didn't have any coffee or tea to offer. In fact she didn't have any drink apart from watery milk which they drank. She had to add equal quantities of water to the milk to make a sufficient quantity for all of them.

She climbed to the second floor, followed by Lucas towards her apartment and rang the doorbell. She didn't know why he insisted on coming to her humble home. Walter opened with a depressed look and downcast eyes.

"What happened to you?" She said, going inside and allowing Lucas to come in too.

"I'm sorry Violet. I didn't mean to but my school shoes tore and fell apart today. I don't have anything to wear to school tomorrow, " he wailed as he turned around. He stared at Lucas standing in their small shabby home wearing a well tailored expensive navy blue suit, exuding a strong aura of power and wealth. He looked at his sister who looked nervous and fidgeted with her hands, not knowing what to do.

"Where's Will?" She asked him, looking around. "Lucas, this is my brother Walter and there's his twin too, William," she introduced. Lucas shook hands with Walter who flashed him a dazzling smile.

"I'm Lucas Parker, " he introduced himself with an amused look on his face.

"Are you Violet's boyfriend?" He asked with a grin.

Violet was too shocked at Walter's question and she cried out in panic, "No, he's my employer, my boss. The owner of the hotel where I work. What's wrong with you?" She glared at Walter.

"No, I'm just asking. Only boyfriend's dropped their girls home," he said, wisely. Lucas's face broke into a chuckle which soon turned into a happy grin.

He leaned towards Walter's ear and whispered, "Soon."

"Hey what are you two whispering about?" Asked Violet glaring at her brother who caught hold of Lucas's hand and pulled him towards his room ignoring Violet.

"You're cool Lucas. You must meet my twin, William," he said, leading him inside his small room which he shared with his twin brother. Violet stared at their retreating backs when Lucas turned to look at her and grinned. He winked mischievously before disappearing inside with Walter.

Violet went up to her room to change for her cafe duty. She hurriedly came out and went to the boys room. Lucas turned towards her, taking in her red short skirt and white top which all waitresses at Lily's Cafe wore.

"Will, run to aunt Mary's and get me some coffee powder and milk," she asked William. He got up to do as asked.

"What for?" Asked Lucas

"Sorry I don't have coffee powder or milk to make you a cup," she said, feeling embarrassed.

"I don't need it. William, stay. Water will do just fine. Please don't get so worked up," he said casually sitting on their beds and looking through their maths text book. Walter went to get him a glass of water and some cookies that uncle Mike got for them.

"Where are you off to?" Lucas asked, looking at her short uniform with disapproval.

"I have a waitress duty at a local cafe from six to nine at night. I'm already ten minutes late, gotto rush. See you," she said, going out.

"Keep it for the last. Now go and apologise, " said Walter. "She works at Lily's cafe. Go straight from here. Take the first right turn and at the end of the road is the cafe. Best of luck," informed Walter.

"Thanks a lot guys," Lucas said, going towards the stairs.

"Will you come tomorrow too Lucas?" Asked William.

"Maybe," Lucas grinned and left. He loved the twins and would love to meet them again. But first he had a job to take care of. Mission Woo Violet.

He started his car and drove as per Walter's directions. He spotted the cafe and parked his car in a dead alley beside the cafe. He strode towards the small cute little cafe, painted in red and white. There were lilies planted in quaint little terracotta pots, lined along the cafe window sills. He opened the door and went inside. It was a small family owned cafe with enough seats for twenty five people. He sat at a table near the window. He looked around for Violet but didn't see her. The cafe wasn't full, only a few people sitting and chatting over steaming cups of coffee and snacks.

A young waitress came inside the cafe and handed him a menu card. She eyed him from head to toe like he was edible and on the menu. "What can I offer you sir?" She asked, leaning down in front of him and pulling her shirt down to show more cleavage through the already open buttons.

Lucas wasn't interested. He didn't even look up at her, while reading the menu card. "I want Violet Nelson. Summon her please," said Lucas.

"She's busy at the back with a customer. She can't come," said the waitress. Lucas's blood boiled. What did she mean? What busy work was she doing at the back with a customer? He stood up and banged his fist on the table.

"I said call her now," he said, angrily and the girl ran inside. The other customers stared at him to see what the matter was.

A haggard looking, dishevelled Violet came out of a door. Her eyes went round with disbelief seeing a furious Lucas standing and shaking with anger.

"What are you doing here?" She asked Lucas. Lucas saw red the moment he saw her. He strode towards her and picked her up on his shoulders and walked towards the exit.

Chapter 5

Chapter Five

"Sir, put me down please. My duty isn't over. They'll deduct wages," she pleaded in a high-pitched voice. She had no idea why Lucas was behaving this way. Her short skirt rode up and she was extremely conscious of tye view that the world was receiving.

Lucas turned a deaf ear to all her pleadings. How dare she service customers for money. He could give her money without wanting anything in return. He was furious. He strode towards his car angrily and opening her car door, he deposited her. Closing the door, he walked into the driver's seat and started the ignition.

"Sir, I'm not going anywhere with you. I told you I need this job," she again repeated with frustration.

"I told you that you won't work here," he ordered angrily, starting the car and driving back to her home.

"Stop the car immediately. What's wrong with a waitress's work? You don't have any problem with my cleaning job at the hotel?" She asked, feeling at her wits end.

"You don't need to service customers at the back, there. So can you explain what the hell you were upto that made your appearance this way?" He asked spitting fire, angry beyond words.

Violet sat dumbstruck and looked at him with her mouth hanging open. What was he implying? That she was a whore who fu*ked customers at the back of the restaurant for money? Anger coursed through her body and she fidgeted with the door handle wanting to jump out of his car.

"Stop this car immediately," she yelled and Lucas stopped, seeing her tremble with anger. "I don't sell myself for money, if that's what you're implying. I would rather commit suicide than do such a thing. I am a waitress not a whore. What made you even think of such a thing about me?" She yelled at him as she tried to open the door.

"So I'm wrong now? Your friend at the cafe said that you were busy at the back with a customer and couldn't meet me. Now tell me I'm wrong?" he said with gritted teeth.

"You're wrong, you're wrong, you're wrong. She said I was busy with a customer at the back but did she say that I was busy fu*king a male customer at the back?" She asked, trembling with anger now. How dare he jump to his own conclusions! She might be poor but she worked very hard for a living.

"It's the same thing," said Lucas, looking at her, feeling a little confused now. Didn't it mean the same thing?

"No it's not. I was with a woman and her sick child at the back in the cafe's washroom. Her child was throwing up and I helped her clean him," she explained, feeling disappointed that now she would lose the cafe job after the scene Lucas created. Many customers had left the cafe and the owners weren't happy.

Lucas stared at her blankly. Was it that simple? Why didn't he think of it before?

Violet opened the car door and ran out and into her building. She trudged up the stairs, sighing. Now she would have to hunt for another part time job nearby. Life couldn't get any worse. How would she manage shoes for Walter after losing a job?

Lucas felt guilty that he uselessly created a scene and made her lose her job. He remembered what she said, vividly.

We skip lunch everyday. If I leave the cafe duty we have to skip dinner too.

He saw her drinking only water today during lunchtime. He had to do something for her. He drove towards his hotel, dejectedly. It was late and Dominic would have left. He would have to talk to him tomorrow for a double pay hike for Violet. She worked very hard and deserved it.

The whole night, he felt restless and upset. How would he apologize to her for his insensitive remarks. He never got worked up for such a trivial thing. Then why did he get so furious at tue thought of another man with her? He wasn't just in love with her. He was hopelessly in love and had no control over himself around her.

This was a new thing for Lucas. He was always in control and exuded power wherever he went. His excessive self confidence and exceptional patience were qualities that his family were proud of. He never lost his shit. He was level headed even in times of crisis. And now this teenage girl made him go so out of control? He couldn't believe himself.

He remembered what her brothers said about her. She really wasn't sny girl. She was Violet, the impossible who made the impossible happen without even having to lift her little dainty finger. She made Lucas Parker fall head over heels in love with her.

He tossed and turned the whole night on his bed. He should have cleared the air with her before returning back.

The next morning, he summoned Dominic early in the morning. Dominic came rushing to see what the matter was. "Yes sir," he asked, standing before Lucas with nervousness

"Mr Evans, I want to know the exact pay Violet Nelson receives for her services at Parker Suites," he asked. Dominic stared at Lucas with nervousness.

"We're paying her 5$ per hour sir," he said gulping with nervousness.

"So less? But the standard is 10$ per hour, isn't it?" He asked surprised that a reputable hotellike Parker Suites was paying so less to a dedicated worker.

"Yes sir. She's inexperienced, so we didn't offer her as per our hotel standards," owned up Dominic, feeling ashamed of himself.

"She might be inexperienced but she's the most hardworking. I want you to increase her salary to 10$ per hour. How much did you offer her for cleaning this penthouse everyday?" He asked and Dominic looked down at his feet.

"I'm waiting for an answer, Mr Evans," he was relentless. He needed to know why Violet had to work two jobs to meet her family's needs.

"She's doing it within her duty hours, so we weren't paying her anything sir," he said in a small voice.

"I don't believe this. Cleaning my apartment isn't part of her duties. I will pay her personally for this work. That would be all Mr Evans. Send Violet up here the moment she comes," he said and Dominic nodded his head.

Dominic went back to his office. Lucas Parker was too interested in Violet, he thought. He seemed obsessed with her. He went about doing the work he gave her.

Lucas waited impatiently for Violet. It was already 9 o'clock in the morning, yet there was no sign of Violet. Didn't Dominic understand that he wanted her to come to his penthouse first thing in the morning? He waited for twenty more minutes and then felt frustrated at Violet for not coming to his penthouse. Was she so angry with him that she couldn't come up to meet him?

He called Sarah,"Mrs Browning, please send Violet up as soon as possible," he said over the intercom.

"Good morning, sir. But Violet hasn't reported to work today," she informed him. Violet didn't come to work? How was that possible?

"I see. Did she call and inform?" He asked curiously.

"No sir," she answered.

"How many leaves did she take so far?" He asked, wanting to know if she were one of those lazy types who bunked work every alternate day.

"Sir this is her first ever since she joined. She preferred leave encashment, sir. So she never took a single leave, " she informed and Lucas thanked her and disconnected the call.

He was concerned and decided to go and see her after the conference that he had to attend.

Chapter 6

Chapter Six

Lucas's conference was postponed to 2 o'clock in the afternoon. So he decided to drop in at Violet's apartment to see her. As he got ready to leave as luck would have it, he received a call from Tyler. He was on his way to LA with his PA, to attend some important meetings. He requested Lucas to receive them at the airport.

Lucas drove his Audi to the airport to receive them. The flight arrived and he greeted Tyler and his beautiful PA, River Ann Wilson. He could see that Tyler was whipped with her already. So he decided to pull his leg and have a little fun at his expense. Tyler didn't talk to him much after the rift that Meredith had created between tthem. Lucas missed the bond they used to share when younger.

After dropping a very pissed off Tyler and his PA at his hotel, he left to shower and get ready for his conference. He was impatient to finish everything and go to see Violet. The conference started forty minutes late and stretched till 4:30 in the afternoon. He returned to his penthouse to freshen up.

Sarah called him urgently on the intercom. Two officers from the Gang and Narcotics department of the Los Angeles Police Department had arrived and arrested one of the guests at their hotel. There was a lot of chaos.

By the time normalcy prevailed, it was 9 o'clock in the night. He dragged himself to his bed to sleep. Tomorrow he had to accompany Tyler to all the Parker Suites of LA for an inspection tour. He sighed thinking about Violet. He would get her number from the employee file and call her. He should have noted it down when Sarah had handed it over to him. He soon dozed off to sleep out of exhaustion.

The next morning, he woke up late. He had to go to Tyler's penthouse at the Parker Suites on Santa Monica beach. He didn't have time to talk to Sarah about Violet or get her number. He decided to meet her when he returned to the hotel. He rushed out to Santa Monica. After the first tour he went to meet the owner of the villa he liked at Santa Monica and fixed the deal. He would consult a lawyer for the legal formalities. He had another meeting with an important client who wanted to have a tie up with their Parker suites for holding conferences.

By the time he was free, it was evening and Tyler invited him for dinner. He could never say no to Tyler. He loved him like an older brother although he only managed to only irk Tyler and pull his leg more.

After dinner, he went back to his hotel to sleep. It was too late to visit Violet anyways.

The next day Tyler and River returned back to Las Vegas. Lucas had grown close to River and approved of her as his sister-in-law. It was obvious that they loved each other. Lucas had to fly to their hotel in San Francisco early the next morning. There was a press conference on their new hotel that had been launched a few days back. The whole day he was busy. He was summoned by his father to Las Vegas by evening to attend the Board of directors meeting the next day. He directly flew from San Francisco to Vegas.

The next morning he went to their Staywell group's head office to attend the meeting. He was twenty minutes early so he sought out River at her cubicle.

"Hi, when did you come to Vegas?" She asked him.

"Last night," he said, looking heartbroken and down.

"What happened to you?" River asked in concern.

"Ann, how do you feel when you're in love?" He asked, looking like a lost puppy. He called River by her middle name.

"Well, you have this uncontrollable wish to be with the one you love all the time," she explained and he nodded.

"And?" He asked curiously.

"And you miss him the moment he's away from you," she continued and Lucas nodded.

"And?" He prodded.

"You want to do it all only with him. Your heart beats faster when you see him. You're in heaven when he kisses you," she said and he nodded enthusiastically.

"Well then, I'm in love," he declared with an excited expression. "Meet me for lunch at Corner cafe downstairs at the ground floor of this building at 1 o'clock. I'll tell you everything." He said and left.

He attended the meeting and it was 1:10 in the afternoon when his meeting ended. Je rushed downstairs to Corner Cafe at the back of the building. He saw River sitting and waiting for him at one of the tables.

"Hey Ann, thanks for coming, " said Lucas as he dragged a chair and sat down in front of her.

"Have you ordered?" He asked her.

"No, I was waiting for you. Let's order," she said, summoning a waitress who checked out Lucas as she approached them. Lucas ordered a burger and fries and she ordered grilled chicken sandwiches.

"So, what did you wish to tell me," she asked after the waitress had left, frustrated that Lucas didn't pay her any attention.

"I'm in deep love with this girl who's just 19 and works as a house-keeping staff at one of our hotels in LA. She's scared of me and won't even look me in the eye. For a month, she'd been cleaning my penthouse leaving a fresh fragrance of violets in my home everyday. I stayed back one day and didn't leave the penthouse to see her and what she did to my home. I've been in love with her after that one encounter. She's elusive and insists on calling me sir. What do I do, Ann? I'll die of heartbreak," he confessed with a deep sigh, holding his heavy head in his hands.

Their food arrived and they started eating. Lucas popped fries into his mouth absentmindedly. "Why is she scared of you? Have you tried anything with her?" She asked in between eating.

"No, I have a bad reputation that I play with women. I really don't. I didn't have any relationship for the last two years and my last hook up was a casual one night stand six months back, before I met her," he wailed.

"Hold on. Tell me how serious are you about her?" She asked him.

"Very. It could marry her right now and be with her forever," he said and River nodded, deep in thought.

"You need to meet her regularly. Once she sees you everyday, she'd be convinced that you're not a monster. Then you can start talking to her. When she opens up, you could get to know her. It's a gradual process Lucas. You can't expect her to jump into your arms overnight," she advised him.

"So what are you suggesting?" He asked, nodding his head in understanding.

"See how you can get to see her everyday. Maybe fix a different time for her cleaning when you're at home. Ask her to make you breakfast too. She could join in and you can make her open up that way. Whatever suits you," she suggested and Lucas's eyes brightened up.

"She's very young Lucas, you have to remember that. Maybe she's totally inexperienced with men. So be careful. One slip of tongue might ruin everything for you, " she said as she finished her sandwich.

Lucas too had finished his burger and fries. They paid and Lucas hugged her. "You're the best sister-in-law ever." He said and she grinned.

"Thanks and update me about what happened. I should get back before Tyler misses me," she said and they grinned at each other.

"He's very possessive about you. He doesn't trust me around you. He thinks I am after you, " he said, unhappily.

"Don't worry, I'll clear the misunderstanding," she said, patting his arm.

"Meredith used to hound me to sleep with her. I never did. But she created this misconception in Tyler's mind, telling him lies and stories about how I slept with her. I swear I didn't but he doesn't trust me anymore, " he told her with a feeling of dismay.

"Everything will be alright, Lucas. I'll clear all misunderstandings when I get the chance," she comforted him.

"Thanks Ann. I love you, you're a dear," he said, giving her a casual hug.

"How dare you?" Boomed Tyler's angry voice as he punched Lucas on the face.

"Tyler it's not what you're thinking. I," she started as Tyler picked her up on his shoulder and walked away towards the door leaving Lucas with a busted lip staring at them in confusion.

"Tyler let me down. I just came here for lunch and to have a talk," she started and saw all eyes upon her, staring at all the drama.

Lucas came running after them. "Bro, listen to me. I was just talking about my own...," he started but Tyler simply dumped her in his car and sped off, leaving an astounded Lucas standing on the pavement.

Chapter 7

Chapter Seven

Lucas felt very displeased with the turn of events. There was nothing he could do for River as Tyler was very possessive about her and wouldn't listen to a word he said. So he decided to return back to LA as his work in Las Vegas was completed.

He flew back to his hotel by afternoon. He contacted his lawyer and completed the legal formalities of buying the villa. It was five in the evening when he got the keys in his hands. He drove towards Violet's house, eager that he could meet her at last. She hadn't come to work for the last few days and he had no idea why.

Coming to a stop in front of her building, he saw a few strange men loitering around, watching him and his car. He went inside the building and up the stairs. What was wrong with Violet? Was she sick?

He climbed to her floor and went to her apartment. His mouth hung open at the state of her apartment. The entire place had been ransacked and destroyed as if a violent tornado went through it. What happened? Where were Violet and her brothers? Were they hurt? He went inside cautiously but saw no sign of them. Panic settled in the pit of his stomach. Were they ok? Dominic had said that her phone was switched off.

"Violet, William, Walter, " he called as he walked around the mess that was their apartment. He was scared by now. What happened to them? He should have cancelled everything and helped them. If only he knew. He prayed that they were alright.

"Violet," he yelled, his panicked voice echoing around the empty apartment. "Walter, please where are you?" He shouted, his voice hoarse with choked tears. Were they alive? Who did this to them? Should he inform the police? "William, I'm Lucas, where are you?" He yelled as a last attempt.

There were no signs of them anywhere. He decided to call the police now. He was about to make a call when the door of the next door apartment slowly creaked open and Walter's scared face peeped out. The moment he saw Lucas, he gasped in surprise.

"Lucas you've come?" He asked as a sob escaped him. Lucas was so relieved to see him that he strode towards Walter and hugged him tightly.

"I had gone out of LA," he informed him, as he stroked his hair to comfort him. "What happened? Where's William and Violet?" He asked a sobbing Walter.

The door opened further and William peeped at him. The moment he realised who had come in search of them, he came rushing out and hugged Lucas too. "Lucas, so glad that you came," he said, as tears filled his eyes too.

"What's going on William?" Asked Lucas, very panicked at their breakdown. Something serious had happened and they needed help.

The door further opened and Mary Jane, their neighbour came out. "I'm Mary Jane Lee, sir. I work as a restaurant manager at your hotel. Please come inside, Violet's with me," she said, inviting Lucas into her three bedroomed apartment.

Lucas walked into her neat apartment in a daze. Where was Violet? He looked around for her. "Come this way," said Mary Jane leading Lucas to a bedroom. He followed her inside and saw that Violet was lying on the bed. He rushed to her side and sat down beside her.

"What happened to her?" He asked in panic? "Violet, it's me? Lucas, look at me?" He pleaded, leaning towards her and touching her forehead.

"She'd been attacked by Lily's son and his gang the morning after her last night of work there. Apparently, customers have stopped visiting their cafe after the incident that night," said Mary Jane. Violet woke up and looked at everyone. "Thankfully Michael, my husband saw them and informed the police. He brought her home. Two of them as well as Lily's son were arrested. So Lily's brother along with the rest of the gang destroyed their apartment. The boys were at my place.

Violet was alone at home and they threatened to abduct her if she went out of the building. Ever since Violet has been getting panic attacks," said Mary Jane.

Lucas listened intently and then saw that Violet had regained her consciousness. He touched her cheek and she looked at him. "I'm here Violet. You want me to punish them?" He asked her and she nodded.

"Good, girl. Now let me call the police. You have to tell them exactly what happened. Will you do that for me?" He asked her gently.

"Yes," she answered. Lucas got up to call the police, but Violet held his hand, refusing to let go, "Please don't go," she said in a scared voice.

Lucas sat down beside her, "Ok, I'm not going anywhere," he said. He called the police and informed them exactly what happened. After a detailed talk, he disconnected the call. "The police will be here in ten minutes. Violet, I want you to get up and accompany me to your apartment and tell the police exactly what happened. Ok?" He asked and she nodded.

Mary Jane sighed heavily, "I tried but she wasn't willing to go to the police," she informed. William and Walter came and sat on the bed beside him too.

"I'm scared, Lucas, " said Walter as he tried to come closer to Lucas. "Me too, will they kill us Lucas?" Asked a scared William.

"No, there's nothing to feel scared of. Let the police arrive and we will tell them everything. They will arrest the culprits and punish them," comforted Lucas.

"Come with me kids. Have some warm milk to soothe your nerves," said Mary Jane as she left the room. The boys followed her out.

Lucas turned to Violet. "Have you eaten?" He asked her.

"I thought you'd never come again," she whispered softly but Lucas heard her distinctly.

"I was out of LA on work. I just returned today," he informed her. She looked down at her hands. Lucas placed his index finger below her chin and forced her to look into his eyes. "Did you want me to come?" He asked, softly.

She nodded as her arms wrapped around his neck and she hugged him close, relieved that he had come after so many days. It was the most innocent hug which brought a tear to his eye. He hugged her close to his body, embedded his face into the crook of her neck. He was so thankful to God that she and her brothers were fine.

"I'm so glad that you all are fine," he said softly and she hugged him tighter. He was lost into the embrace.

"Lucas, the police are here," announced Walter as he came into the room with William.

Lucas released Violet and tried to compose himself. Walter grinned at him, "I hope you haven't told her you love her?" He whispered but it echoed in the quiet room and everyone heard it. Violet's eyes widened as she blushed to the roots of her hair.

"No, not yet. Should I?" Lucas asked him with a chuckle.

"No, silly, you say it later," suggested William.

"Guide me, ok? It's my first time," Lucas said with a naughty grin as he winked at Violet and left the room to deal with the police. He was glad that Violet was reacting to him. He wanted to make her comfortable with him and help her regain her confidence.

Violet glared at William and Walter as they giggled naughtily and rushed out to oversee the grown up affairs such as dealing with the police. They went and stood with Lucas as he talked to the police.

Violet couldn't help the blush that wasn't disappearing. Could some-one like Lucas really love her? Was it true or was he just fooling around with her brothers? She was very confused.

Mary Jane appeared at the door. "Violet, Lucas wants you to go and talk to the police," she said, coming forward and helping her get up.

Violet walked slowly towards the door. She hadn't been able to eat well after the trauma and was feeling too weak. Mary Jane helped her go to her apartment where Lucas was standing with Michael, three police officers and her brothers.

"There she is, officer," said Lucas, holding her around the shoulders and bringing her close to the group.

"Violet, these are officers Brian Larson, Greg Foster and Jon Macmillan from the LA police department. Tell them what happened exactly," he instructed her.

"Please come inside and sit down, officers. Violet's too weak to stand for so long," said Mary Jane and every one agreed and went inside Mary Jane's living room to sit.

"Start from the beginning, Miss Nelson," said officer Macmillan.

Chapter 8

Chapter Eight

"Lucas and I had a misunderstanding and he carried me out of Lily's cafe to his car. He wanted me to discontinue at Lily's cafe, so I left my job that night. The next day, I went to the cafe to get my previous month's salary but they denied me. They said that I drove away all their customers because of the drama that I caused. So they didn't pay me anything. I was returning home when the owner Lily Hudson's son, Tony attacked me with his gang of goons," said Violet, looking down as she remembered it all.

"Then? Did they harm you?" Asked officer Larson.

"They gagged me and carried me to a van. I struggled with all the strength I had in me. They threatened to rape me. I was frightened out of my mind, officer. It was then that Michael and his colleagues saw me while going to work. They saved me and called the police. Tony and two of his gang members were arrested. The rest escaped. Michael brought me home," said Violet.

Lucas stared at her, listening to every word intently. He was thankful that Michael saw her and could save her just on time.

"Then?" Prompted officer Foster.

"In the evening, my brothers had come here to this apartment and I was alone at home cooking dinner. Lily's brother Adam came with five men. They trashed my entire apartment, shredded the clothes, ransacked and destroyed every possible thing they could see. I tried to stop them but they beat me up too. They threatened me that if I stepped out of the building they would abduct me. They warned me against involving the police. They also told me to forget all my dues," she told them.

"Firstly, we want you to help us file an FIR against them, Miss Nelson," said officer Macmillan. Violet agreed and they filed an FIR against Adam, Tony and Lily. The officers entered the details and two of them got up and went to her apartment and took photographs. They took down Lily's address and names of the men involved in the crimes.

"We're calling in more officers to arrest all these people at the earliest. I will station two officers here for your security," said officer Foster.

"I'm taking Violet and her family away with me, officer," informed Lucas and the officer nodded.

"Sure Mr Parker. Just give me your details so that I can update you about the case," he said and Lucas gave him his business card. The officers went away and Lucas looked at Violet. It was already 8 o'clock at night.

"Is there anything intact that you can pack? I'm taking all three of you away with me to my penthouse tonight. Tomorrow we will decide what to do next. It's not safe to live here alone anymore. Even after the arrests are made, they would somehow get out on a bail and then take revenge," said Lucas.

Violet couldn't decide what to do. She couldn't live with Mary Jane forever. In fact now Mary Jane and her family too were in danger for helping her out.

"I can't leave Mary Jane, Michael and Emmett alone here to face their wrath," said Violet, looking down at her hands.

"Mrs Lee, would you like to shift to the hotel's staff housing in downtown LA or continue living here?" Lucas asked Mary Jane and her husband.

"Actually sir my husband works at a departmental store here as a cashier. it doesn't pay well. He's looking for a better job. Once he gets, we can afford to go to a better neighbourhood," said Mary Jane.

"There's an urgent vacancy at the hotel for a stockroom manager. Why don't you apply Michael? It pays better being a managerial position. You can shift to the hotel's staff housing for the time being and then shift to your own place later. Is this apartment your own?" Asked Lucas.

"No sir, this is rented," informed Mary Jane.

"Yes, sir. I will do that. Thank you, " said Michael with a smile as their son came to sit beside him.

Lucas looked at the boys. "William, Walter, come with me. Let's check out what we can retrieve from your apartment and pack it all up. You all are coming with me and that's final," he ordered, looking at Violet who stared at him wordlessly.

She wanted to go with him. She was too scared to live alone here but Lucas was her employer and a billionaire. Why was he doing so much for them? What was his interest? Did he really love her? She was too confused to decide.

Lucas and the boys went to their apartment to pack and she too got up and went after them. There wasn't much left to pack. A few clothes that were saved from their attack, the file of important papers that was inside the old safe at the backside of the closet. A few books and stuff of the boys. A family photograph of their parents and grandparents. A suitcase full was all they could salvage.

They hugged Mary Jane and Michael. The boys hugged their friend Emmett. "How will I walk barefoot, Lucas?" Asked Walter, suddenly realizing that his only pair of shoes were torn.

Mary Jane smiled and went inside. She came out with an old pair of shoes that belonged to Emmett. "Wear these," she said.

"Thank you aunt Mary, " said Walter, eagerly wearing them. Violet slipped on her work shoes which were intact and William wore his school shoes. They locked the apartment and thanked Mary Jane and Michael and went down the stairs to Lucas's car.

"Wow, this is such a cool car, Lucas. I too want to grow up and look after a hotel," said Walter, running his fingers along the smooth body of his Jaguar XF which shone in the bright street lights.

Lucas chuckled and opened the back door for the boys to climb in. He opened the front passenger door and ushered Violet inside. He could see that she was not her usual self. She was confused and scared. He loaded their suitcase and opened the driver's seat and climbed in.

The boys were busy admiring the car and inspecting it. Lucas looked at Violet and touched her soft cheek in a light caress. "Don't worry so much, " he advised her. Lucas noticed that she trembled at his touch. He was excited that he could convince her to go with him.

Tonight it was already late, so he would take them to his penthouse. Tomorrow he would have his new home on Santa Monica beach cleaned and they would all shift there.

He drove to the hotel and parked his car. They all clambered out of the car. Lucas unloaded their suitcase and they all entered his private elevator. Violet could feel all eyes upon her. She felt very self conscious. She knew that tomorrow she would be the hot topic of discussion. Every body would talk horrible things about her. There'd be lots of malicious gossip.

"It's no big deal. Let them talk," said Lucas and Violet looked at him with surprise. How did he know what she was thinking?

"Wow Lucas, is this place yours?" Asked William looking down from the glass capsule elevator.

"Yeah," he answered with a small smile.

"Can we live here forever? We'd eat out at the hotel everyday. Best life ever," said Walter, rubbing his growling tummy. "I'm already hungry. Can we eat dinner? Last few days at aunt Mary's we had the best dinner ever. Otherwise we eat bread and water and milk," said Walter.

"What type of dinner is that?" Asked Lucas, perplexed.

"Add water to milk and have it with bread," answered William with a grin. Violet glared at them. "Shut up, you two," she reprimanded.

They reached the penthouse and Lucas led them inside. He called room service and ordered dinner. "This is huge, Lucas. It's as big as a stadium. You live all alone here?" Asked William, looking around in awe.

"Yeah, I live alone. What else to do? I don't have anyone to call my own," Lucas answered, staring at Violet. Their eyes met and time stood still as he held her gaze daring her to look away.

He was glad that the twins announced his feelings for her. It would have taken him ages to confess to her that he loved her. Now he would do his best to prove to her that he loved her.

"Poor Lucas," said Walter and Lucas laughed. The magic was broken and Violet looked away.

"Well, dinner should be here in five minutes. Why don't you all freshen up?" He asked them and the boys looked very excited at the mention of food. He felt bad that they couldn't afford a nice meal while there was so much food wasted at the hotel everyday. He should do something about this. Maybe save the spare food and distribute it to the homeless on the streets.

He showed the boys a spare bedroom where they could wash their hands. "You both can sleep here," he announced and they jumped with joy.

"And Violet?" Asked Walter.

Chapter 9

Chapter Nine

B efore Lucas could answer, the doorbell rang and Lucas went to
get it. Their food had arrived and the boys came rushing out.

They inhaled the heavenly aroma of food. "Let's eat, what are we
waiting for?" Asked an excited William while Walter started checking
out the dishes.

"Violet eat before everything goes into our tummies, " said Walter.

Lucas chuckled at their enthusiasm. Violet came out quietly and
smiled at her brothers. Lucas saw that she had a sad expression in her
face. He knew something was troubling her and he had to speak to
her.

"Eat Violet, " he said and she nodded, sitting at the table.

They all served themselves whatever they wanted to eat. Chicken in
white sauce, mushroom rice, potato wedges, mixed vegetable stir fry
and cream cheese lemon cake.

"This is awesome Lucas. Do you eat this everyday?" Asked Walter, incredulously.

"Yeah but I don't like it. I like home cooked food," he said and the boys looked at him like he had grown two horns.

"Violet, you don't like the food?" Asked William, seeing her just sitting and staring at the food.

"Yeah, it's very good. Thank you Lucas," she said. "It's late, finish your food fast and go to bed both of you, " she said. The boys nodded. They fought over the same piece of chicken which they both wanted. Lucas intervened and halved the same piece and gave each of them a halve.

At last dinner was over and they all cleaned up everything. Violet stored the leftovers in the refrigerator while Lucas rinsed the used dishes. "Where will Violet sleep, Lucas?" asked William.

"I'll show her to the bedroom next to mine," he said, wiping his hands.

The boys raced to their bedroom,"Goodnight Violet, goodnight Lucas," they chorused.

"Come I'll show you to your room," said Lucas, turning towards Violet. He walked to the bedroom next to his. "You can sleep here. Your suitcase is here. If you need more clothes, I can lend you mine, " he said gently. Violet nodded,"Thanks, I have some, I think I can manage," she said, with a shy smile.

"Goodnight Violet," he said, staring at her face longingly. What could he do to get a kiss from her? He longed to hold her in his arms. To ask her what was bothering her. To comfort her but didn't know how to approach her.

"Goodnight sir," she answered and he winced. It seemed as if she wanted to remind him of her position.

He would have to deal with it. She couldn't continue to call him 'sir'. He would go crazy. He walked to his bedroom feeling more frustrated than before. He thought that he was making progress, that she had started opening up to him. Now it seemed that they were back at square one.

Lucas couldn't sleep. With Violet just on the other side of the wall, he was restless to hold her and comfort her. He tossed and turned and eventually gave up. Getting up he went to get a bottle of water from the kitchen.

He quietly made it to the kitchen and came out with a bottle of water. His eyes went towards the huge floor to ceiling windows near the far end of the living room where a huge 8 seater sofa was placed to watch the night skyline. The silhouette of a woman could be seen clearly against the window in the dim lights. Violet? What was she doing here?

Lucas walked towards the silhouette. He saw Violet standing and quietly watching the stars in the sky. "Violet, what are you doing here?" He asked her, staring at her radiant face glowing in the moon-light.

"Searching for mom, " she said, going and sitting on the sofa. "She's a star now. She died last year in an accident. I can't pull any more," she said looking into her lap.

Lucas sat down beside her. "Tell me what's bothering you?" He asked.

"I don't want to be a burden on you sir. Tomorrow we will go back to our apartment. I need to join work too. The boys have to rejoin school," said Violet with a sigh.

"You're not going back to that apartment, " Lucas said firmly.

"It's my home. How long can we run away? We will deal with whatever happens. I can't live here with you forever, free of cost. I can't take advantage of your kindness, " said Violet. Lucas was more frustrated at her stubbornness. How would he convince her that she was all he wanted? How would he tell her that he wanted her to stay with him forever?

"I have bought a new house on Santa Monica beach. Tomorrow we will shift there. The boys can go to the community school nearby and you can work at our hotel in Santa Monica. Or you could work at my house. I would have to search for a housekeeper anyways. So you can instead take care of the house and cook for us. That way you wouldn't be living free of cost. What do you say?" He asked her.

She seemed to think about his proposal. In fact she liked the fact that she didn't need to work in this hotel anymore. She would be bombarded with questions and back bitching if she continued.

"Can I answer tomorrow, sir? I need to think about it," she said and he nodded.

"Take your time," he said looking at her with concern. Would she accept or decline?

"Lucas," he said, still staring at her. She turned to look at him.

"I beg your pardon?" She said, not getting what he said. She was deep in thought, considering his proposal.

"I said, call me Lucas," he repeated. His gaze, not leaving her beautiful face. It looked so fresh, innocent and young from so close. The pink top clung to her body and made her look so delicious and creamy white in the moonlight. He could see the soft mounds of her breasts from the neckline of her top. Her plump red lips looked freshly bitten as if she had been biting it thoughtfully.

"Let's keep it professional, please. I need to work for you," she insisted.

"No, I don't want to keep it professional," he told her and she looked at his agitated face.

"I don't do flings, " she said quietly, looking again at the stars.

"I love you, believe me it's not a fling," he said and she looked at him in disbelief.

"Why?" She asked.

"I don't know," he said. He picked up her hand and placed it on his chest. She felt his wild heartbeats and gasped. "See? It's beating only for you," he whispered. Violet snatched her hand away as if stung. She felt goosebumps on her skin at his touch.

"I don't want a physical relationship," she told him. Maybe he wanted her for a night to warm his bed. Why else would a billionaire like him say such things to a poor cleaner of his hotel?

Lucas got up as if stung by her words, "I don't need to lie to get a woman in bed. I love you. Why is it so difficult to believe?" He asked, and turning, he strode off to his bedroom and closed his door.

Violet sat in the dark, confused and undecided. Maybe he did love her after all. He really didn't need excuses and lies to get a woman. With his looks and money no woman would be able to resist him. She got up and went to her room. Curling up on her bed, she dozed off to sleep.

Chapter 10

Chapter Ten

Next morning Violet woke up early and took a shower. She had decided that she would go to Lucas's Santa Monica house and start afresh. At least it was better than going back to her apartment and living in constant fear.

She made some coffee and sat down sipping the delicious delicacy. She didn't have any beverage at her humble home and getting to sip coffee in the morning was a luxury for her.

Lucas came in and sat down with his head lying down on the table. She went to get him coffee. Placing the coffee in front of him, she sat down to sip her own. He looked at his coffee and sipped, avoiding looking at her. She felt guilty for hurting him.

"Lucas, I'm sorry," she said, sincerely, feeling bad for her own insecurities. Lucas stared at her as if he couldn't believe his own ears.

"What did you say?" He asked, incredulously.

"I said I'm sorry, " she repeated, looking into his blue eyes.

"No before that," he prompted. He wanted to hear her say his name again.

"Lucas," she said as her cheeks reddened and she lowered her eyes to her coffee. Lucas was bowled over by her cuteness. A smile tugged at the corner of his mouth. He felt so deliriously happy that he wanted to pull her into his arms.

Suddenly Walter and William came rushing out of their room and came racing to the table. "I win," said William as he reached the table first and sat down.

"You cheated, I was peeing and you started racing," said Walter, glaring at William who laughed heartily. Lucas chuckled at the two. They were like a tornado.

Violet glared at them, "Behave, you two. I'll get you your milk," she said, getting up.

"Why can't we have coffee like Lucas?" Asked Walter, eyeing his coffee.

"Because you both are children, " she explained and walked away.

"No, we're not," said Walter and glared at his sister's retreating back. "Lucas can you give me a sip of your coffee, please?" He asked in a whisper.

"Sure, " said Lucas, amused.

"Me too, please," said William.

They took a sip of his sugarless bitter coffee and stuck their tongues out like puppies. "Yuk, yuk, yuk. How do you drink it?" Said William. Walter went to rinse his mouth. Lucas laughed out loud.

Violet came with their milk and biscuits. "What's wrong with you two? Did you eat a frog?" She asked, looking at them.

"A frog would be better than that, I guess," said William and Walter agreed.

Violet rolled her eyes and handed them their glasses.

"Now I'll be going to my new villa in Santa Monica to get the house cleaned and ready for us. We'll shift there by afternoon," announced Lucas and the boys stared at him with excitement.

"Are we shifting to a new house today?" Asked Walter, curiously.

"Yes, on the beach, " informed Lucas with a smile.

"Oh boy! I've never lived on a beach in my life," said William, his eyes dancing with excitement. "Can we go with you please?"

"We can clean very well. Please Lucas, " pleaded Walter.

Lucas looked at Violet seeking permission to take them. "If you three are going, what will I do here alone? I can help with the cleaning, " she offered.

"You don't need to clean. I'll hire people to do it. You need to regain your strength first," said Lucas looking at her. He was so excited that she changed her decision to return back to her apartment.

"Yay, we're going to the beach," sang Walter as they raced to the kitchen to deposit their milk glasses.

They came out and stopped for a second. "Can we take a shower, Violet?" Asked William and Violet nodded.

"No playing with water," she warned and they raced to their room.

"Will you help me pack Violet? Then we can go to our new home as soon as we're done," said Lucas. Violet nodded and picked up their mugs and went to the kitchen. Lucas called room service to order their breakfast.

He then called the affordable housing complex that Parker Suites had reserved for its employees. There were two units available. He went to the kitchen to inform Violet. "There are two units available at the affordable housing complex that I was talking about. Here's the number of the caretaker. Inform Mary Jane to contact here immediately," he said, handing Violet the number scribbled on a piece of paper.

"Thanks. You think about everyone, " she appreciated.

"No, only about you," he said. She could feel him close behind her. She could feel his hard chest brush with her back and she shivered at the touch. His hot breath fanned her neck.

"I'm glad that you decided to stay with me," he said, staring at her creamy neck. He wanted to skim his lips along the smooth skin of her neck.

"Let's pack," she said, turning around to go to his room pack but he didn't budge an inch. She looked up into his dark eyes staring down at her. His hands on either side of her, holding the kitchen sink, trapping her. He stared fixedly at her upturned face and neck and felt himself go crazy with the wish to kiss her.

"Lucas," she called again. He still didn't move away. She placed her hands on his chest to push him away. She could drown in his blue eyes if not careful. They were a beautiful shade of blue and they pulled her to him, "Lucas, we need to pack," she said, trying to think of an excuse to escape. She couldn't afford to fall for him.

His eyes looked at her lips with deep longing and then abruptly he left her and walked away to his room, slamming the door shut. Violet stood transfixed to the spot. Should she go and pack his stuff?

He did ask, didn't he? She went up to his room and opened the door and went inside. She closed the door and turned around and came face to face with a shirtless Lucas. His muscular, lean hard body, his tight abs and v-line all resembled some Greek God. She blushed and looked down at her feet.

"I'm sorry, I came to help you pack. I'll come some other time," she said, turning to go. His arm went around her and he pulled her flush against his bare chest. She gasped at being crushed to himself.

"Why do you always try to escape me? Don't you like me even 1%?" He asked with pain in his eyes.

"I I, it's not that. There can't be anything between us, Lucas," she said, trying to escape from his hold. She wanted to feel his love, stay in his arms forever but she was scared. What if he got over her and decided that he didn't want her anymore? She wouldn't be able to survive that heartache. So it's better not to fall for billionaires.

"Do you like me?" He asked, pulling her closer. His face inches away from hers as he stared at her lips. She looked down.

"Please understand Lucas. I can't afford a relationship, I have a lot of responsibilities," she told him, feeling very dejected that she could not listen to her heart.

"I can share your responsibilities, Violet, " he said and she stared at him. She wanted to be loved and cherished by him. She wanted to stay in the sanctity of his arms. "Tell me do you like me?" He repeated.

"Yes," she said softly and he smashed his lips to hers in a hungry and passionate kiss.

Chapter 11

Chapter Eleven

B efore he could deepen the kiss and taste her sweet mouth, footsteps came running up to his door and Walter and William pounded on it.

"Lucas, Lucas, someone's at the door. Come quickly, " they yelled. Lucas left her reluctantly and opened the door.

The boys looked at their sister and Lucas and grinned. Walter pulled Lucas's head to his ear,"Lucas did you kiss her?" He asked in a whisper.

Lucas grinned shyly, scratching the back of his head. He pulled a shirt on and left with them. "Please could you pack whatever you want me to wear?" He said with a wink. Violet rolled her eyes and went to check his closet.

The boys whispered amongst themselves as they left the room with Lucas. By the time they all returned, Violet already had packed two suitcases full of his stuff. He came inside the walk in closet and smiled happily. "You're fast. I think I should keep you with me," he said with a wink. Violet blushed remembering the way he had kissed her. The feeling of his lips still lingered on hers. The truth was that she was very disappointed when he broke the kiss. It was her first kiss and it ended abruptly.

Lucas brought another suitcase and emptied his important stuff from a safety deposit box. He too helped Violet as the boys checked out his TV in his room. Inside the walk in closet, Lucas came near her and whispered into her ear, his lips skimming her earlobe,"I will continue where we left off." She turned and looked at him with shock. Her brothers were in the next room and he was thinking of kissing her?

"No," she whispered back, her eyes wide with horror. Lucas grinned and continued packing. He would have to finish that kiss properly. After tasting her mouth, he was wild with the desire to completely ravish her mouth.

He carried all the suitcases outside the closet to his room. "Walter, go and call Billy here," he instructed. Walter nodded and went to call him.

"William go get your suitcase," said Lucas and William ran to get it. He got it after a minute. Walter came back a minute later with a tall buff man.

"Billy, this is Violet. Violet this is my right handed man Billy Preston," introduced Lucas and Billy nodded at Violet in acknowledgement. Violet smiled a hello. "Billy, please take all these luggage to my new home. The housekeeping team from the hotel should be there cleaning. Oversee the work. We're on our way there," Lucas instructed.

"Yes sir," said Billy and picked up all the luggage and left.

"Are we ready to go?" Asked Lucas.

"Yes, let's go, yay," said William.

Lucas glanced at Violet and she nodded. "Fine then, let's lock this up and leave," he said.

So they checked everything and locked all windows and picked up their important stuffs and walked out of the penthouse. "Should I inform Sarah ma'am before leaving?" Asked Violet.

"Yes, I informed her. They have calculated your last month's dues and will pay you when you go," said Lucas. Violet grinned happily and went downstairs to Sarah's office. Lucas and the boys went down to the parking lot and waited beside his car. While the boys admired his car, Lucas spoke to Billy on the phone.

After twenty minutes, Violet came down with a smile on her face. She received a lot of money and she was happy.

"Let's go," she grinned and Lucas smiled back at her enthusiasm. He helped her to the passenger seat while the boys bundled into the backseat.

"Are we there yet?" Asked the eager boys for the tenth time.

"No," said Violet, "Why don't you look for all blue things and count? Whoever sees the most will win," she said to engage them.

They drove along Santa Monica Ocean Avenue to Hart street which was just a stroll away from Main St, Santa Monica Pier, and Venice Beach. The boys jumped with excitement as Lucas drove through the open gates into the garage. They all piled out of the car.

The boys ran to the boundary iron railings and watched the beautiful ocean beyond. There was a huge park beside their house and the kids jumped excitedly at everything. "Lucas there's an outdoor shower for rinsing off after an ocean swim in the rear yard. Come see it," said Walter excitedly.

"You check it out, I'll just check out the cleaning. Later we will explore. Ok?" said Lucas.

"Sure," Walter said, running off to discover more things.

"Don't go to the oceanfront alone. Whatever you do, stay in the house," warned Violet and the boys nodded before disappearing behind the house.

Lucas led Violet inside the house where workers were cleaning and sanitizing the entire house. Billy came downstairs and updated them. The cleaning of the upper floors were nearly over and they would soon shift to the lower floors.

Violet left them to talk and went to check out the house. The house had a stunning open-plan great room with hardwood light floors, a huge fireplace, a wrap around balcony, and beautiful ocean views from the huge bay windows. Overlooking the great room was an airy loft which instantly became her favourite place to sit and watch the stunning Pacific views. On the ground level was a large entertainment and dining room with its own kitchenette, deck, and additional back entrance. The deck was an extension of the wrap around balcony and the beautiful seating area made it her favourite too. She inspected the kitchen. She had never seen so many modern appliances in all her life. She had to learn to operate all of them.

Violet was already in love with the house. Lucas came to stand beside her,"You like it?" He asked, looking at her and coming close to her. He had bought it with her on his mind. He wanted to live with her forever in this little haven.

"Yes, I love it, " she answered shyly.

Lucas's arm went around her and he whispered in her ear,"I want to live here with you, forever," he said biting her ear lobe, teasing her senses.

Violet shivered at the torture, "Forever is a dream, Lucas, " she said honestly.

"No, it's not. You can't escape from me. I want nothing less than a forever with you, " he said and Violet looked at him, feeling lost in the promises he was making. She wanted to give in to him and see what the future held. She was tired of fighting this feeling for Lucas.

She wanted him to kiss her. She wanted to believe that he truly loved her. Maybe she would deal with heartache when it struck.

"I want to kiss you Violet, " he confessed, his lips skimming her neck and inhaling her soft sweet scent of violets. "Do you want me?" He asked, deliriously.

"Not now please," she said, eyes widening as she looked all around her. The workers, Billy or the boys might come in any minute.

"Just tell me, do you want me to kiss you," he asked and she nodded shyly and walked away, rushing up the stairs to see the bedrooms.

Chapter 12

Chapter Twelve

Violet climbed up the stairs just as the cleaners completed their job on the top floor. Billy accompanied them downstairs, "Upstairs done ma'am. Please would you check?" He said courteously.

"Yes, thank you, " she said, feeling on top of the world. She had never received so much respect in her entire life. She thanked the workers too and went to check.

Violet loved the luxurious top floor with it's spacious master bedroom with a large walk-in closet and marble tile bath. The room opened to a private balcony offering stunning views of the ocean.

"You like this room?" Asked Lucas, coming up behind her.

"Yeah, it's yours," she said, rushing out to check another room.

"Only for the time being," he declared, following her out. She blushed crimson at his implication.

She came to a room which was smaller and looked very feminine and cosy. "This one's mine," she declared. Lucas grinned at her," Sure," he said, walking away, whistling a tune.

Violet looked at the room but couldn't understand what made him so happy. She went downstairs where Lucas and the twins were excitedly looking at two adjoining rooms.

"Please Lucas let these be ours," pleaded Walter.

"No, you are too young to stay downstairs all by yourselves, " said Lucas, strictly.

"Pretty please? We promise we won't do anything without your permission. Please Lucas, say yes," pleaded William.

"You will escape to the ocean on your own and we wouldn't even know. No, you will share a room upstairs, " said Lucas.

"We swear we will never go alone without your permission. Please Lucas, " said Walter, with tears in his eyes. Lucas sighed heavily and looked at Violet who stood at the door, observing them quietly. She was overwhelmed by Lucas's concern about the wellbeing and safety of her brothers.

"Ok, you can stay here," she said and they jumped with joy.

It took the worker another hour to complete the downstairs cleaning. Lucas paid them well and they left satisfied.

Violet went to the kitchen. They had forgotten to eat breakfast in their haste and were ravenous. She decided to make some spaghetti bolognese for lunch. Lucas and the boys went with Billy to get grocery and other necessary stuff. She didn't have anything to cook till they returned. So she went up to her room.

She checked out the ensuite, it was so welcoming with a bathtub to soak in. She went to a door that opened to a balcony. Going out, she loved the view of the ocean. Turning around she headed back to her room but was confused. There were two doors instead of one. One led to her room. Where did the other one lead to?

She opened it and saw that it led to Lucas's room. So they shared a common balcony. She smiled and went back to her room. She would have to keep her room locked now at all times. She went downstairs and took a walk around the house, checking out the lawns and the flowering plants, the outside shower head, the sit-out on the deck outside the entertainment room. It all looked like a dream house to her. She couldn't believe that she could be so lucky to live like a princess in such a house.

She thought about everything that Lucas had done for her and her brothers. There wasn't any condition for his help. He helped them because he wanted to. He had bonded with her brothers deep from his soul. There was no drama or fakeness about it. He was as genuine as the sun and the universe. She liked him more than she should. So should she give him a chance? Yes.

She felt much happier at the decision her heart wanted to hear. She hummed a happy tune as she walked on the grassy lawns, barefooted and free.

Lucas's car returned with the twins excitedly chatting with him. She was glad that the twins bonded so well with Lucas. His car came to a stop and the twins excitedly clambered out. Billy too got out and unloaded the bags of stuff that they had bought.

"Violet come quick. We've got lunch. Lucas said you will rest today," said William. Violet smiled at Lucas who took her in, barefooted and standing on the grassy lawns. He got down from his car and approached her.

"Loving it?" He asked, coming closer.

"Yes," she said, looking down at her feet. It had been ages since she'd done this.

"And me? Will you give me a chance?" He asked with a wink.

Violet smiled at him and walked towards the house,"C'mon boys, let's eat, " she said to the twins.

"What about my answer?" Lucas yelled after her.

"Maybe," she said, turning and looking at him. Then she chased the twins inside the house. Lucas stood like a statue. Was she giving him a chance? He couldn't believe his own ears. He had to be sure.

He followed them inside with a smile. Billy too grinned hearing their conversation. Lucas couldn't wait to get her alone. He wanted her in his arms. He wanted his kiss.

"Lucas hurry. The food will disappear into our stomachs. This is the best food ever," said William, stuffing a slice of pepperoni pizza into his mouth.

Violet handed a box of pizza to Billy as he was about to leave,"This is for you, Billy," she said.

"You can go back to the hotel, Billy. I will call if I need you," said Lucas.

"Thank you, sir, ma'am," Billy said, accepting the box of pizza from Violet. He waved at the boys and left on his motorcycle to Parker Suites, Santa Monica where he worked.

They enjoyed their meal. "Tomorrow, we will check out the schools in the neighbourhood and get you admitted," Lucas said and the boys looked at him with a bored expression.

"So soon?" Asked Walter. Violet glared at him.

"Yes, so soon," she said strictly. The boys kept their plates in the kitchen and washed their hands. Then they picked up big bags of stuff and ran to their rooms.

"What are inside those?" She asked Lucas, curiously.

"Clothes, toiletries, shoes and other stuff for the boys," he informed, finishing his pizza.

"So many? I would have bought them what they needed," she said, looking at Lucas with disma. They made him spend so much.

"No big deal. They can't roam around without clothes. I've got stuff for you too," he said, pointing towards three big shopping bags full of things for her.

Violet looked at him, "Why did you spend so much on us?" She asked.

"You don't want clothes? I don't mind you staying naked. I would want you to if we were alone, " he said, with a mischievous smile. Violet's eyes widened in shock. What a shameless man! She picked up the empty pizza boxes and plates and escaped to the kitchen. The sound of Lucas's chuckle followed her inside.

She dumped them into the huge dustbin. She washed the plates and dried them. Arranging them where they belonged, she walked out of the kitchen. Lucas was nowhere to be found. She just picked up the shopping bags and went up to her room.

She sat and arranged the clothes, accessories, lingerie and shoes and toiletries in their respective places. How did he know her exact size? She blushed crimson at the thought. Going out of the walk-in closet, she collided with Lucas's chest. Was he watching her arrange her lingerie and blush?

"What were you thinking?" He asked, his arm going around her waist as he pulled her closer, her body crushed to his.

"Nothing," she said, blushing more.

"I want my kiss, Violet, " he said, his hand going to her hair and holding her head. He lowered his head and hungrily claimed her lips.

Chapter 13

Chapter Thirteen

Lucas was glad to get her alone in her room at last. He had been dying to taste her lips ever since he was interrupted in the morning. He pulled her roughly against himself, probing into her lips with his tongue. She opened her mouth inviting him to taste her sweetness. He needed to taste her thoroughly. His tongue entered her mouth and battled aggressively with hers. He bit her lips and she bit him back. It was the most erotic kiss that he had ever experienced.

He groaned with the need to taste more of her. She kissed him back the same way he did and he drowned into her warmth. Nobody had ever left him so breathless as Violet's inexperienced kiss did. He broke the kiss to breathe.

"Violet, where are you? We want to goto the park next to our house. Please can we?" Shouted William as he came up the stairs towards her room. Lucas left her immediately and went out of her walk-in closet to her balcony.

He didn't want the twins to see him in her room. He had to do something about this situation soon. He didn't want to continue to steal kisses from her like someone doing unauthorized stuff. He wanted her to be only his, legally and wholeheartedly. He needed to marry her soon. For his mental health as well as physical wellbeing.

Violet fixed herself and came out of her closet to see William looking at her room with awe. "This is so cool, Violet, " he said.

"Isn't it?" Asked Violet excitedly. "So, what did you want?"

"Please Violet. We want to go play in the park nearby and then see the ocean from near, " said William.

"Ok, call Lucas. We'll all go," she said with a smile.

"Yay, thank you, thank you, thank you, " he said, rushing next door to convince Lucas. They both came out laughing after five minutes.

Violet accompanied them downstairs where Walter was waiting for them, buttoning up his new shirt. He wore his new shoes and the moment he saw Violet, he jumped up and down like a Jack in the box.

"Violet, look Lucas bought me new shoes," he said, wiggling his leg at her.

"Wow, it's awesome. Did you thank Lucas?" She asked him.

"Yes, I did but Lucas said he only needs hugs. So I hugged him. He bought stuff for you too. Did you hug him too, Violet?" Asked Walter with a naughty glint in his eye.

Lucas looked at Walter and shook his head,"What? I'm helping you to get your girl, " said Walter and William smacked his arm.

"Lucas can get her on his own," said William, and they communicated through some strange sign language that Violet didn't understand but Lucas chuckled.

"What's going on?" Asked Violet perplexed.

"Nothing, just that Lucas smells like you," said William and Violet's jaws dropped as she looked at Lucas with pink cheeks. Lucas laughed out loud.

"Are we going or not?" Asked Lucas and the twins raced to the main gate. Violet and Lucas walked together with the twins racing ahead of them to the park. Lucas tried to hold her hand but she didn't. Not with those two and their loud mouths.

"They need to get used to seeing us together," said Lucas, feeling frustrated.

"Oh," said Violet and Lucas caught her hand and held it in a tight grip, not leaving her.

"You're mine and everyone here should know that," he declared. Violet looked around to see lots of children playing around, birds chirping on the branches of the trees, squirrels running from tree to tree and rabbits peering from behind the bushes.

She looked at Lucas incredulously, "Everyone, who?" She asked him.

He looked around too and then grinned,"Whatever, " he said and they laughed.

They sat on a bench and William came to call him. "Lucas, play football with us please," he requested.

"Sure," he said and then looked at Violet and gestured to her to watch him play. Violet rolled her eyes.

They were happily playing and more children had joined them in what seemed to be a pretty interesting match. Violet walked away slowly to the beach.

Life has changed drastically the day she met Lucas. He came into her life like a whirlwind and turned her life upside down. He brought with him happiness, laughter, freedom, luxury, comfort, enjoyment. Everything that was missing in her life. Few days back she was an overworked cleaner at a hotel, juggling between two jobs on an empty stomach. She didn't have time for such little pleasures. Walking on the beach had been a distant dream.

Lucas made her feel secure, loved and happy. She wanted to believe that his love for her would remain forever. That she would be happily married to Lucas. She watched him play with the kids, laughing, cheating, winning, typical Lucas. The children beat him and chased him. It was mad fun. They loved him. He had this quality in him which attracted everyone to his personality. He exuded so much warmth and care that people wanted to be with him. Just like she wanted to be with him. Just like she loved him.

She stared back at the ocean and heaved a huge sigh. She loved him? Yes. The realisation made her feel scared. How could one love another in such a short span of time? Only in movies but it was the hard truth. She loved him and only him. When the liking she felt for him turned into love, she had no idea.

"Thinking of me?" Whispered Lucas as he came up behind her. His arm went around her waist and he pulled her back against his chest. She rested her head on his chest.

"Not at all. I was just admiring the beauty of it all," she lied, feeling a blush spread on her face and neck. The sun was setting and it cast a beautiful orange red hue all around. The beach stood out pale while the ocean waters reflected the light of the setting sun. It was a magical world.

"And thinking of me. How I'll kiss you again at night? How shall I make you moan out my name?" He said, planting a kiss below her earlobe.

"Lucas the twins. What are you doing?" She said, looking at the twins busy playing.

"Loving you and taking what is mine," he said, possessively.

The twins raced to the beach and played for sometime. Then they all returned back. It was a much needed relaxation that they all needed.

Violet made spaghetti bolognese and baked a simple classic jam and cream victoria sponge sandwich cake with raspberry fillings.

"Yum, this is the best cake ever," said Walter.

"Yeah, I could eat it everyday. You're the best baker, Violet, " said William.

"Seriously this is better than the ones I bought so far. You should start a bakery, Violet," said Lucas.

"Thanks, " said Violet. Their comments made her think hard. Should she start a bakery in the neighbourhood? It was better than being a cleaner. She smiled satisfied that she had found her identity at last. She was a baker and would do everything to make it a success.

Chapter 14

Chapter Fourteen

V iolet completed her work in the kitchen. Lucas had locked the house well before going upstairs to his bedroom. He ensured that the boys were nicely tucked in bed too. Violet went to William's room and opened the connecting door to Walter's room.

"Good night Will," she said,"If you both want you can sleep with each other in the night," she said before leaving for Walter's room. William also jumped up and went with her.

"Good night Walt. You both can sleep together if you want to. Don't go out at night. The door has an alarm system. Don't touch it," she warned both of them.

"Yes Violet. Don't worry," said William.

"Violet, do you like Lucas?" Asker Walter.

"Yes, now sleep, " said Violet with a smile.

"Will you marry him? Then we can live here forever," asked Walter.

"No Walter. That's not the reason why I'll marry him. If I marry, it'll only be for love," she confessed.

"You can't love Lucas? He's so lovable," asked William.

"Quiet now and sleep both of you," she said, blushing.

"Silly Violet loves him already," said Walter and they both grinned. Violet smiled shyly and left them to go upstairs to her bedroom. She remembered what Lucas told her before,

I'll kiss you again at nightHow shall I make you moan out my name?

She wanted him to kiss her. She wanted to explore these new feelings with him. She went to her room and straight to shower. Showering and feeling fresh, she went to her closet to get into something to wear to sleep. She had forgotten her old sleepwear at the hotel today in the morning. She smacked her forehead and searched amongst the clothes that Lucas got for her. There were only two revealing babydolls. She hunted further and found a lilac cami and matching shorts set. She happily put it on, relieved that she didn't have to wear those babydolls.

"I knew you would wear these, " said Lucas as he sat on her bed, patiently waiting for her.

Violet gaped at him wordlessly. How did he come inside? She had locked her room.

"How did you come inside?" She asked him, looking at the unlocked balcony door. She remembered locking it though.

"I have a key, you know. You really can't lock me out, " he said with a wink.

"That's not fair, " said Violet. He had a key to her room? It wasn't acceptable. What about her privacy?

"Everything's fair in love, " he said, stretching and holding her hand. He pulled her onto his lap. "I told you I want to kiss you again, " he murmured, kissing the base of her throat. She arched her throat to give him more access. Lucas loved her eagerness, it made him tingle with excitement as he kissed all over her neck, inching towards her creamy jawline and then her delicious mouth.

"I love you more than words can say," he whispered against her skin, making a delicious shudder run down her spine. He captured her mouth in a sensuous and passionate kiss. Her arms went into his soft silky hair, tugging his head close to hers. She opened her mouth to his waiting tongue to do wonders to her mouth. Lucas deepened the kiss and a moan escaped her.

His hands moulded her body into his own, fusing them together. She felt strange sensations in her body which only yearned to be touched by him. His hands bunched at her hips and he pulled her close. His body was on fire and he was too aroused to feel anything else. Her kisses alone made him hunger more for her. She could feel his arousal poking into her. It made her throb with want. She felt wet and aroused for the first time in her life.

His mouth left hers and sucked her neck while his hands explored her body. The soft, this camisole top did nothing to hide her body from his wandering hands. He pulled the top and his hand went underneath it to caress her bare breasts. She had already discarded her bra to sleep.

His sharp intake of breath as he touched her hard peaks was enough to know that he was on the verge of losing control. "I want you so bad, Violet," he whispered.

He knew that she was just a teenager. He didn't want to rush her into committing herself to him. He wanted her to grow, mature and then discover herself and come to him of her own free will.

He arranged her clothes properly and picked her up in his arms. He opened her door and carried her towards his own room. "Where are you taking me Lucas?" She whispered.

"To my bed where you belong," he answered her.

"I I'm not ready Lucas, " she stammered. She didn't want to do anything serious with him yet. She wanted to know him more. She wanted to discover herself more, explore her true feelings more.

"I know. We can just hold each other and sleep. Can't we?" he asked her gently.

"Yes, I want to, " she owned up.

"Me too," he said. He carried her to his bed and deposited her on it. He climbed in too and lay down behind her. He spooned her from behind, "Sleep," he whispered and she smiled.

They soon dozed off in the comfort of each other's arms.

The next morning, Lucas and Violet took the boys to a school within walking distance from their house. "Lucas, I can't afford this," said Violet.

"Yes we can. You will soon start earning too. This school's nearby and the boys can walk home," said Lucas, strictly, not willing to listen to her.

She would have to think of starting her bakery soon. She would have to first inform Lucas before taking any step. So they completed the formalities and enrolled the boys. The twins were ecstatic to see such a big school with so many opportunities and activities. Their school would start from the next day and they went to the administrative office to get their books and stationery.

"Thank you, Lucas, " the twins chorused as they went home together.

Violet noticed that there were no bakeries nearby and outlets for baked goodies too. "I want to start a bakery here in this neighbourhood, Lucas," she said and everyone looked at her with admiration.

"That's a wonderful decision. You draw up a menu and we will make some printed ads and give out in the neighbourhood. Billy could slip it in everyone's mailbox. Let's see the response. If the response is good we can rent a small shop also, " he said and Violet grinned.

She kissed his cheek, "Thank you, " she said. The twins too grinned happily.

Chapter 15

Chapter Fifteen

L ucas went to work and Violet cleaned the house, cooked and did the laundry. The boys were busy checking out their new books and stationery.

When free, Violet sat down to draw up a menu plan. She included a comprehensive menu plan including sweet as well as salted savouries, cakes and desserts. She named her bakery, Violet's Delights. She made design templates for her promotional ad pamphlets to be distributed.

It was nearly evening and Violet sat with the boys as they went through their books. "Violet, what are reflexive pronouns?" Asked William.

"Show me the book?" Said Violet. She read the paragraph and explained, "Reflexive pronouns are words that are used when the subject and the object of a sentence are the same. For example, I believe in myself. Here myself and I denote the same person, so myself is a reflexive pronoun. The nine English reflexive pronouns are myself, yourself, himself, herself, oneself, itself, ourselves, yourselves, and themselves. Understood?" She asked.

"Yes. Then see this sentence? Here, itself should be the reflexive pronoun. Right?" Asked Walter as he solved an exercise in a rough sheet.

"You're a pretty good teacher too, Violet. Tell me what you cannot do," said Lucas, looking at her with appreciation.

He strode into the room with three women accompanying him. One of them was literally hanging from his arm. They had heavy makeup on their faces and designer expensive clothes. The smell of their strong perfumes filled the air as they walked in wearing stilettos. They looked down their noses at Violet with disgust.

"Violet meet, Miranda, Vanessa and Leilani. They were my old school and college friends and came down to my hotel for a party today. Ladies, this is Violet, and those are Walter and William," he introduced and the woman on his arm, Leilani looked at her with malice in her eyes.

"I'll have a lemonade. What about you girls?" Asked Leilani to her friends.

"Same as you," they chorused.

"You, get us lemonade," Leilani ordered Violet.

Violet's face fell. She got up to go to the kitchen. "I'll help you Violet, " said Lucas, following her to the kitchen. Violet made the lemonade silently. Lucas took the tray of drinks to the women. He didn't like the way they treated Violet but he knew Leilani and her bitchy ways. He had always tried to stay away from her clutches. She pursued him like an obsessed witch all her life. He hated the sight of her. He knew that she could stoop to any level.

He didn't wish to meet them ever but they had other plans and forcefully followed him all the way to his house. He wanted to introduce Violet as his girlfriend but thought against it with the fear that Leilani could create misunderstandings. Violet was too innocent to see through her bitchy lies. He just wanted them to leave but to his dismay, they stayed till late.

"Ask your maid to serve us dinner," said Leilani, trying to sit as close to Lucas as possible.

"She's not my maid," corrected Lucas, moving away from her. After making their lemonade, Violet had retired to her room and didn't come down. The twins went to their rooms and locked themselves inside. They hated it that Lucas's guests misbehaved with their sister and Lucas just watched, not saying a word to them.

"Whatever, your housekeeper, then," said Leilani. Lucas went to the kitchen and served them the dinner Violet had cooked. "You should throw her out Luca if you have to do all her work, " said Leilani in her nasal tone. Her friends agreed and they laughed and talked about how worthless servants had become nowadays. Lucas silently sat with them, thinking when the torture would end and they would disappear.

"Ladies, I have an early morning flight tomorrow, let's wind up here tonight?" Asked Lucas and they all agreed.

"Where are you going, Luca honey?" Asked Leilani.

"Europe tour," answered Lucas. He had to check out some of their hotels in Europe and although he didn't wish to go, he had no choice. It was a two week ordeal and he didn't want to stay away from Violet. If the twins didn't have school, he would have taken all of them with him.

The women left at last swearing to catch up with him once he returned back. Lucas sigher with relief and went to the boys room to see that they had gone to sleep on an empty stomach without eating any dinner. Feeling awful, he closed and locked the main door and went upstairs to Violet's room.

She opened the door, he face pale and quiet, her eyes sad, as she waited for him to speak. "I have an early morning flight tomorrow. I'm going away for two weeks on a Europe tour," he said, waiting for her to react. When she didn't say a word, he continued, "Let the twins go to school. Here, take my card for any expenses that you may need," he said, handing her his card. He took her mobile phone from her hand and punched in Billy's number.

"That's Billy's number. Call him whenever you need help," he said, handing her phone back.

Lucas was confused by her behaviour. She didn't say a word when he declared that he was going away. Did she not like him at all? He nodded and went away to his room.

Violet softly closed her door. She had heard everything that Leilani spoke about her. The truth was Lucas didn't once inform them that she wasn't a maid or a housekeeper here. She was confused. Was she a housekeeper here? Who was she to Lucas? A friend? A housekeeper? A new toy? Or a maid?

Silent tears streamed down her cheeks as she thought about Lucas. When he had such beautiful and rich friends, why would he love an ordinary teenage girl like her?

She woke up and went downstairs to make coffee. She found a note from Lucas beside the coffee machine. It read,

Leaving now. Stay safe. Call Billy you need him. Use my card. Lucas

She sat and sipped her coffee. It was just six in the morning. Lucas left an hour ago. He didn't even kiss her goodbye. Did he go with those women who came last night? The thought made her blind with jealousy.

She tried to put all thoughts of them behind her as she proceeded to take a shower and then make breakfast. The twins had school and would wake up anytime soon. By 9 o'clock in the morning, Billy came to take the twins to school since it was their first day.

She cleaned Lucas's room as well as the twins rooms. She made lunch for the boys and walked about the empty house, missing Lucas.

She picked up her apartment keys and thought of hiring someone to have it cleaned. She would talk to Billy when he came in the afternoon. She called Mary Jane and had a chat with her.

It seemed that all the culprits had been arrested and Mary Jane shifted with her family to the hotel's affordable housing complex two days back. As she disconnected the phone, the twins came home. Walter came rushing inside.

"Where's Billy?" She asked him.

"He got a call from the hotel, so he left," said Walter.

"Come outside quickly, Violet. Those bad women have come again," said William, rushing inside the living room.

Chapter 16

Chapter Sixteen

V iolet followed them outside to see Leilani and her friends lounging in the living room. The moment she saw her, she lashed out,"You, get us something to drink. Just because Lucas is away don't think you can laze around," she said in a sarcastic tone spewing venom at her.

"You get your own drink. Why should I?" Said Violet angrily.

"How dare you talk back?" Said Leilani suddenly springing up and slapping Violet hard.

Walter went inside to call Billy, but he wasn't picking up his phone.

"How dare you hit my sister?" Said William, going ahead and stamping her heel clad foot. She yelped in pain.

"Get out of Lucas's house, you shameless bitch. Take your scoundrels with you," said Leilani as her friends helped her sit down.

"You three get out of here. This is our house. Lucas wants me to stay here and I'm not going anywhere else," said Violet, stubbornly.

Leilani and her friends laughed out loud. "Lucas brought you here? To be what? His whore for a week? See this ring on my finger?" She said, showing a ring on her ring finger. "I'm his fiancée. He will come back to me after he has his fun with you. Did he fu*k you yet?" She asked with a laugh. Her friends too laughed heartily.

"It's not what you think. We both love each other," said Violet.

"Oh, he told you that? He tells that to everyone. One fu*k and all the love will fly out of the window. Believe me. I've known him all my life. He comes back to me everytime. Don't believe me? Ask his mom," she said with a smug expression.

Violet's heart broke. She was confused. His mom knew Leilani? Violet realised that Lucas never introduced her to his family. He never told her much about himself. He never asked her to be his girlfriend or fiancée. He just brought her here and told her he loved her. What did it all mean?

"Lucas asked me to come and live here in his absence and that's what I'll do. You are welcome to continue to work as a maid. If not, get lost from this house. I, as his fiancée will not tolerate lazy workers, " said Leilani.

Violet stood transfixed to the spot. Lucas asked her to stay here? He didn't mention anything yesterday. "I don't believe you. Lucas would have told me that you would be arriving here. You're lying," she said. William went inside to check with the phone.

"You don't believe me?" Laughed all three of them, at her. Leilani produced a piece of paper. "See this? It's a pregnancy report. I'm pregnant with Lucas's baby. Now you know why he wants me to stay here? He doesn't want anything to do with you three anymore. He is too much of a gentleman to tell that to your face. So now pack up and get lost," said Leilani with a victorious smile on her face.

A sob escaped Violet as she realised the truth. Lucas couldn't tell her last night so he left abruptly without even a goodbye kiss. His fiancée was pregnant and he didn't want to play around with poor, available women like herself anymore. She ran inside and picked up her handbag with her necessary stuff. She went to the twins rooms and started packing their stuff. The things that they brought with them.

The twins didn't say a word. They heard everything that Leilani said. They had tried to call Billy fourteen times, yet he didn't pick up their call. They went out of their rooms and out of the main door quietly. Violet had the money she received from her hotel. She called a cab and all of them trooped inside. The cab sped off when Billy's motorcycle came to a stop in front of the gate. He watched the can drive away. Who was it that went away in a cab? He decided to go inside and check. Why were there fourteen missed calls from Violet's number?

Violet and the twins reached south LA, to their humble home in W Crest Boulevard. William and Walter helped unload the luggage while Violet paid the cab driver. No one spoke a word about what happened. The twins knew that Violet was too upset to discuss anything. So they left the topic and decided to face the situation bravely.

Violet opened the door to the mess that was strewn all around the apartment. "Let's clean up whatever we can," said Violet. The twins nodded and everyone started cleaning up.

"I'll get some food items to cook. I'll be back soon. Lock the door and clean up as much as you can," she instructed them and they nodded.

"Be careful, Violet, " said William. Violet nodded and left.

Violet went to the nearby shopping centre and bought a few food items. She couldn't splurge with the limited money she had. Without a job, she had to spend stringently.

She tried to block the words that Leilani told her. She tried to forget everything. She didn't want to cry. She knew all along that it was a dream, that Lucas could never really love her. She brought this heartbreak upon herself. Billionaires never fell in love with their cleaners. It happened only in fairy tales. She walked back home.

The harsh reality hit her that she was jobless and too heartbroken to think straight. How would she pull herself together and support her family? She had no idea. Teardrops fell from her eyes as she looked down and walked home as fast as her legs could carry her. She cried for the love that she felt for Lucas. Did he lie to her? Did he not feel anything for her?

Why did he come into her life? She was surviving somehow with two jobs and a roof over her head. Now she saw no way to overcome the state her heart and mind was in. She had lost everything.

If it weren't for the twins, she would have ended her wretched life. She trudged back up the stairs to her apartment.

She opened the door with her keys and saw that the twins had cleared a lot of the trash. She set about cleaning the entire apartment with them.

It was evening by the time they had brought some order to the apartment. Violet made some some beef stew and they had it with bread for dinner. The twins went to their room to sleep. Violet cleaned the kitchen and went to her room.

She took a shower and changed into torn cotton nightsuit. It was the only thing she had. Tears uncontrollably streamed down her cheeks and she broke down into her pillow.

"I don't want to live without you Lucas," she repeated again and again as she broke down helplessly, sobs wracking her small, delicate frame.

Chapter 17

Chapter Seventeen

The next morning, the three of them sat at the small table near the kitchen.

"We can all go to the departmental store to work, Violet. Don't lose hope," said Walter. They could see that Violet had completely lost faith in herself.

"No, I will go to the departmental store and search for work. If I get work, I will enrol you both in your old school, next week, " she said, looking down at her hands. She should have been firm in her decisions. One false step had her family in such a situation.

The twins nodded. They didn't want to argue and add to her worries. She gave them their old breakfast of bread and watery milk and went out to the departmental store in the neighbourhood.

"We need salespeople to guide and handle customers. Can you do it?" Asked the strict manager in charge, Mr James Howard.

"Yes sir, I can," she said confidently.

"Look, you don't have the required qualifications or experience but we will hire you since your mother used to work here. But your initial pay will be less than what we pay our salespeople. Once you prove us your worth in the first three months, we will increase your pay. Are you willing to join?" He asked her.

"Yes sir. When do I start?" She asked him.

"Tomorrow morning at 8 o'clock, " he said and she thanked him and left. The pay was the same as what she was getting at Parker Suites. She was satisfied that after three months they would increase her pay.

She returned home and smiled at the twins and told them the happy news. They hugged her and all three of them discreetly wiped their own tears. Violet tried to keep herself busy to avoid all thoughts of Lucas out of her head. It was an impossible task though as all her heart and mind did was miss him, his smile, his touch, his kisses, the way he looked at her, the way he spoke to her, everything.

She ran to her bedroom every now and then compose herself and try to control the tears that spilled out every time. The day went by slowly and she just couldn't wait for it to get over. She was eager to join work tomorrow. At least it would keep her busy and she could just drown herself in work. Thankfully the day came to an end and she dragged herself to bed.

The next morning, she made breakfast and served the twins. She made lunch for them to eat when she was away. "Don't open the door to anyone. Stay inside and do whatever you want. Here's mom's old phone. If you want you can call me anytime you want on my mobile phone, " she said.

The boys nodded, "Don't worry, Violet. We're big boys. We will study and stay at home, " said William.

Violet left for work. The whole day she was busy with different types of customers and dealt with different situations. She didn't get time to sit. She worked four hours overtime for the extra pay. The manager was very happy with her. She came home, tired and haggard. The twins made sandwiches for all three of them. They had it for dinner and went to bed.

Violet went to work the next two days. She had the overtime pay paid to her daily. With money in her hands, she decided to enrol the twins to their old school on Monday. It was Friday already and she had a leave the next day. She did five hours overtime and left the store happily with the extra money.

Going towards her apartment, she thought of cooking something better for the twins tonight. A commotion nearby made her look up. A huge group of local people had gathered around a luxurious black sleek Cadillac Escalade parked right opposite her apartment door. A uniformed chauffeur was leaning against it.

Whose car was that? Lucas didn't possess a Cadillac. Neither did he have a chauffeur. He preferred to drive himself. But if not Lucas, then who? She approached her main door and looked up. Everyone was peering at the car and the commotion it created from their balconies and windows.

"Excuse me. Are you Violet Nelson?" Asked a male voice from behind her. She whirled around and saw a young man, a year or two older than her, wearing a pair of denims and a branded sports tee shirt standing behind her. He smelled of expensive perfume and cologne. His branded expensive sunglasses were casually dangling from his pocket.

"Yes, how do you know me?" She asked. The man grinned at her heaving a sigh of relief. He looked back at the car and gestured with his hands. The door opened and a beautiful brunette, with long silky hair and brilliant blue dazzling eyes came out. She wore a pair of black denims and a red tee shirt. She grinned at her too.

"Found her?" she asked the man with a smile of relief.

Violet looked from one to the other. Who were they? They looked familiar. Did she know them? The woman looked at her and smiled,"I'm Serenity Parker, Lucas's younger sister and this is Liam, our youngest sibling," she introduced. Violet stared at her with her jaws dropped to the floor. What were Lucas's siblings doing here? Did they come to insult her just like his fiancée? She looked at them with wide, round eyes.

"Sera, you're scaring her. Hi, you look too young to be with bro. Are you an adult?" Asked Liam, looking at Violet with mischief as Serenity punched his arm.

Violet blushed at his question. "I'm nineteen, okay," she answered, rolling her eyes.

"Aww. Now I've found someone younger than myself. We can all pull her legs, Sera," he said and received another punch.

"Shut up, " said Serenity. "Violet, don't mind him. He's dumb. Look, we need to talk. Can we go up to your apartment?" She asked and Liam glared at his sister. Big sisters were a bully.

"Sure, come this way," said Violet, leading up to her apartment. She opened the door and led them inside. Walter and William came rushing out of their rooms to see who came into their home. They all sat down, "They are my brothers, Walter and William," she said. "Boys, this is Lucas's sister, Serenity and his brother, Liam," she introduced.

"Hi," the boys chorused and Serenity waved at them and Liam shook hands with them.

"What did you want to talk about?" Asked Violet apprehensively.

All of you need to pack and come with us to Las Vegas, " said Serenity with a lot of seriousness.

"Why should we?" Asked Violet in confusion.

"Because mom wants you to. She sent us to fetch you," said Liam, trying to make her see sense but Violet was more confused than ever. Why would Lucas's mom want her? Did Leilani complain about her?

"Why?" She whispered in a scared voice. "What have I done?"

"You have committed a crime," said Liam with a serious face. Serenity smacked him in his biceps. Violet looked at both of them with a scared expression. She couldn't think of any crime that she'd committed.

"I swear upon God that I haven't done anything, " she said to them in a panic stricken tone.

Chapter Eighteen

"I'm just kidding, relax. I meant you've committed the crime of stealing bro's heart," said Liam, winking at Violet. Violet stared at him in surprise. Then her cheeks coloured profusely as realisation struck.

"Why do I need to go to Las Vegas?" She asked, her young, innocent face so wild with worry that Serenity took pity on her.

"It's ok, don't be scared. Lucas got into a fight with our cousin Tyler in Paris. Both landed at the hospital. Dad brought him to our home in Las Vegas yesterday. But he wont eat, rest or give us any peace. He wanted to come and get you. He has made our lives hell. Mom is tired of him. So she sent us to get you so that he leaves us in peace," informed Serenity.

"Lucas was in hospital? Is he ok? What happened to him?" Asked Violet as big fat tears cascaded down her cheeks.

"He's fine now. He only needs rest. Why don't you three pack and come along with us? You can see him for yourself. Our flight is in an hour," said Liam.

"There's nothing to pack actually. All our stuff has been destroyed after an attack," said Violet, getting up. The boys too got up with her.

"We know. Lucas told us. I've asked Billy to get your stuff from the Santa Monica house and reach the airport in half an hour," informed Serenity.

"Then let me freshen up and we can leave," said Violet excitedly. She was so happy to be able to go and see Lucas. The news that he loved her so much brought a spring to her step. She quickly went to her bedroom and freshened up. She collected their essential stuff and locked up the apartment well and left with the others.

It was 6 o'clock in the evening. They reached the airport in twenty minutes. Billy was waiting for them already. They rushed with the check-in and boarded the flight. The twins were excited to travel in an airplane for the first time in their lives. Walter smiled at Violet.

"Are you happy now Violet? See Lucas really loves you," he said and Violet smiled shyly.

Serenity, who sat beside them smiled at them too. "Don't pay any heed to Leilani. We all hate her, especially mom. She has been after Lucas since their sophomore year. Lucas hates her. He escaped from

Las Vegas because of her. That engagement ring as well as the pregnancy report, all are fake," Serenity said.

"How did you know what Leilani said to me?" Asked Violet in confusion. There weren't anyone at the house at that moment apart from Leilani and her friends and Violet, William and Walter. Then who could have informed Lucas?

"As you left Billy came in and saw you leaving. He cornered Leilani and threatened her. She left with her friends, sensing trouble. Then he played the CCTV footage of the camera near the staircase. It had recorded the conversation that took place that day. Billy informed Lucas. But Lucas saw the message only after he was released from the hospital. He wanted to come and get you but dad brought him home. He's not in a position to travel much," said Serenity, with a smile.

Violet grinned happily. So Leilani was lying after all. Her Lucas really loved her. "I can see why he's so whipped with you. You're so cute and just like an open book. It's so easy to read you, dear," Serenity said and winked at Walter.

Walter grinned too while Violet blushed crimson. Violet learnt so much about their family, about Lucas's parents and so much about him. "He's very level headed and patient. He never behaved this way before. He's very hard to impress actually. Girls always swarmed around him. This is the first time he's been behaving this way. He's become angry, impatient and impossible. He loves you a lot Violet.

You're very lucky that he cares so deeply about you. Don't ever doubt his feelings for you," said Serenity.

"I won't. I'm convinced. Sorry for causing so much trouble, " said Violet, feeling bad that they had to drop everything and run after her. She was glad however that they did. She had lost all hope of living.

"Not at all. Anything for Lucas. He's done a lot for everyone. He's the backbone of the family actually. Mom dotes on him actually. You'll see," said Serenity. Violet smiled at the knowledge. So he was loved by all. "In fact we're all glad that he's chosen you and not Leilani," informed Serenity with a grin.

They were served dinner and they hungrily tucked into the delicious food.

They reached Lucas's huge white stone mansion by 9:40 in the night. It was like a grand palace with a huge tiled courtyard in the front. A sparkling fountain with a marble statue of Apollo adorned the entrance. The lights around illuminated the entire mansion complex with adjacent buildings nicely interconnected around a sprawling swimming pool.

Serenity led her to the backside, to a building beside the swimming pool, followed by the twins and Liam. A maid ushered them inside. She brought their luggage inside.

"This is Lucas's house. Mom and dad live in the main building. I live in the opposite one and Liam lives in the one next to mine," she informed Violet. Violet stared at the luxuriously decorated all white and sparkling interiors. She had never seen anything so exquisitely beautiful in her life. Even the boys were too quiet, staring with wide eyes at Lucas's house.

"He should be in his bedroom. Come, I'll take you, " said Serenity.

"I think I'll wait here," said Violet, suddenly feeling shy.

An aged couple entered laughing at some joke from the door on the opposite side. The woman looked very sophisticated with her dark chocolate brown hair fixed up into a French twist. She wore a light blue sheath dress and still looked extremely beautiful. Her eyes looked like Serenity's and her nose resembled Liam's. The moment she noticed Violet's wide eyed stare, her face relaxed into an easy smile.

"Welcome home, Violet. I'm Eugene, Lucas's mom. Are you eighteen yet, dear?" She asked, with concern.

"Thank you, for having me here, Mrs Parker. Yes, I'm nineteen," she answered with a shy smile. "These are Walter and William, my brothers, " she introduced them.

"Oh, just call me mom. This is Lucas's dad, Eric," she said as Lucas's dad approached them with a smile.

"Hello, sir," she said extending her hand for a shake. But Lucas's dad hugged her instead.

"Call me dad, dear. So the torture ends," he said with a smile. "Welcome home," he said to Violet and patted the twin's heads.

"Did you all have dinner?" Asked Lucas's mom to Serenity.

"Yes mom. I just need to sleep. Happy? We've done your job," said Serenity.

"Take Violet to see Lucas. The twins can sleep in the room next to mine. Come children," she said to them.

The boys went to Lucas's mom. Liam grinned and with a wink left towards his building. Lucas's dad walked with the twins, chatting with them while leading them towards the main building.

"Don't worry about them. They will sleep in Lucas and Liam's childhood room next to mine. It's huge with so many things to play with that they wouldn't miss you at all. I'll take good care of them. You meet that crazy son of mine. He hasn't eaten anything, by the way. I'm sending his dinner. Feed him something if you can," said Lucas's mom as she winked and left.

Serenity rolled her eyes. "All the best sweetheart, I wouldn't want to be in your shoes, right now," she said. "Let me take you to the lion's den."

Chapter 19

Chapter Nineteen

S erenity led Violet up the stairs to what seemed to be Lucas's bedroom. Violet's heart thundered in her chest as she looked at the closed door. She was too excited to meet Lucas. She couldn't wait to be in his arms. Serenity opened the door and called Lucas.

"Lucas wake up," she said to Lucas lying sprawled on the bed.

"Go away, I don't want to wake up," mumbled Lucas with his head embedded in the pillow.

"Seen who I've got," Serenity continued.

"No, I'm not interested. Go away, " he said without looking up.

Violet peeked into the room and saw his shirtless body in the bed, wearing only a pair of sweatpants, riding low. She blushed, looking away. Serenity quirked her eyebrows at her and she blushed more.

"Ok, look up and see at least," she coaxed, as she pushed Violet inside his room. Lucas uncovered an eye and looked towards the door.

He gasped and sat up. "Violet?" He whispered, with shock. "How ddid you come here?"

"I brought her and her brothers silly, " said Serenity. "Ok now you both catch up. I'm off to sleep." She said, shutting the door.

Lucas got down from the bed and limped towards her. Violet rushed towards him. "Are you hurt?" She asked, touching his arm.

"A little. I'm very hurt here," he said, staring at her and pointing at his heart. "Why did you leave Violet? Don't you trust me? Don't you have any faith in my love?" He asked in a pained voice.

Violet went close to him and brushed the hair gently off his face. She held his cheek,"I'm sorry. I do now. I'll never leave you, " she said. Lucas's arm went around her waist and he pulled her close to his chest. Violet laid her head on his bare chest, closing her eyes. She'd come home to Lucas and would stay with him forever.

Lucas kissed her forehead and then her neck. He pulled her face close to his and lowered his head and smashed his lips to hers in a soul stirring, wild kiss. His tongue plunged into her open mouth eagerly tasting her, playing roughly with hers. She kissed him back too and when she bit his lips, he groaned with pleasure.

"I love you, Violet," he confessed as he broke the kiss to catch his breath.

"I love you too, Lucas, " she whispered and Lucas looked at her with surprise.

"You love me?" He asked with wonder.

"Yes, very much," she said, hugging him tightly and placing a kiss on his neck. His whole body shivered with excitement.

A knock on his door brought them apart. "I'll get it," said Violet, going to the door. The maid had brought Lucas's dinner. Violet took it from her hands and thanked her. She closed the door and placed it on a coffee table in his room.

"Come and eat, Lucas, " she said but Lucas shook his head.

"Only if you feed me," he said stubbornly like a child.

"Yes, I will feed you. Please come," she insisted. She went and held his arm and brought him towards the loveseat in his room. She made him sit and sat down beside him. She fed him lovingly as he stared at her without wavering an eyelid. Soon the food was finished and Violet was satisfied. She kissed his cheek and he groaned.

"That won't do Violet. I want to make love to you again and again. I want you naked and moaning under me," he said as he pulled her onto his lap. Violet gasped at what he said.

"Aren't you hurt?" She asked, hesitantly.

"You're my drug. If I don't have you, I'll be more sick. I want to be inside you, Violet. I'm tired of aching for you. I can't control myself anymore. Let me ravish you," he said against her lips and he captured them again, in a passionate and possessive kiss, branding her with his teeth, sucking her, biting her and making her only his.

She too kissed him back with equal fervour. She had missed Lucas so much in the last three days, craved his love in fact. Lucas was on fire, his whole body was out of control needing Violet like a drug. He pulled her closer to his body, moulding her to himself, thrusting and grinding his huge arousal against her.

"See what you do to me, Violet. I'm aching to be inside you, " he said, breaking the kiss, his voice husky and hoarse with desire.

"Then make love to me Lucas. I want you to," she whispered as she sucked a spot on his neck. He groaned as his body shuddered with need. He picked her up, her legs going around his waist. He held her hips possessively as he strode towards the bed.

"Are you hurt, Lucas?" She asked him, concerned.

"No, I'm fine," he said, as he looked at her with dark eyes.

Depositing her on the bed, his eyes lustily stared at her with deep hunger. He pulled his sweatpants down exposing his naked body for her to feast on. Violet was mesmerised by his sculpted body, his bulging hard biceps, his muscular chest, his eight pack abs, his sinfully sexy v-line, his thick muscular legs all made him extremely drool worthy and drop dead gorgeous. He was very well endowed and she could see how aroused he really was for her.

"Touch me please," he said, coming on the bed and hovering over her body, supporting himself on one elbow. The other hand caught her hand and placed it on his heart. A hiss of satisfaction escaped his mouth as her soft creamy hand touched his body, stroking down his hard torso, abs and v-line to his massive arousal. She stroked the full length of his arousal and he closed his eyes and groaned in pleasure. Then he caught her hands and stopped her.

"If you continue any further I'll cum right now into your hands," he said with a smile tugging at his lips. He never had to struggle so much to keep sane. Her one inexperienced touch had him literally release it all.

"I want to see you, Violet, all of you," he said, pulling her top over her head and discarding it. He unclasped her bra and pulled it out and threw it away. His eyes grew darker and his pupils dilated seeing her creamy full breasts. She was untouched and innocent, he could see and it made him all the more aroused to think that he was so privileged to be able to have her all to himself. His hands touched her breasts intimately making her moan in pleasure.

He immediately latched onto them one at a time, sucking like a baby, teasing with his tongue and kneading with his hand. His other hand went downwards and unbuttoned her denims and pulled it down her body along with her panties. His hand touched her intimately, feeling her wet heavenly folds as Violet moaned with the throbbing pleasures that she was experiencing for the first time. He pushed a finger inside her and thrust in and out.

Violet caught his hair and the bedsheet with the other to cope with the pleasures that he was giving her. He thrust another finger and she was trembling with he need to release. "Cum for me, Violet, " he whispered in a raspy voice full of lust.

She released all her juices onto his waiting hands and he licked them clean. His mouth left her breasts and went down to where his fingers were playing havoc with her body. He sucked her wet folds, making her cum for the second time.

"Are you ready for me, baby?" He asked gently, positioning himself above her.

"Yes," she whispered and he entered her in one thrust. They made love many times during the night. Lucas was insatiable where she was concerned.

They slept in each others arms in the wee hours of the night.

Chapter 20

Chapter Twenty

The next morning, Violet woke up too sore to get up from the bed. Lucas chuckled and carried her to the en-suite. He had prepared a warm bath for her. He placed her on the counter and captured her lips passionately.

His hands explored her naked body, touching intimately everywhere. "That's it. I'm marrying you today and I won't change my mind," he stated.

Violet stared wordlessly at him. He's planning to get married today? How was it possible? Then she remembered that he was Lucas. Anything was possible for him.

"Today? Will everyone agree?" She asked him hesitantly.

"They have to. They have no choice," he said, picking her up and climbing into the tub like she didn't weigh anything.

He sat down in the tub and pulled her on top of himself. Gasp escaped her as he entered her gently. He captured her lips as he thrust inside her gently, making love in the bathtub. The warm water soothed her body and the pain healed a lot. Lucas couldn't stop. This was all he ever wanted. Her. Now that he had a taste of her, he couldn't stop. His mind only revolved around her and how he could make love to her endlessly.

He couldn't take the risk of being away from her again. So he bathed her and dried her. Then drying himself, he wrapped a towel around his waist. He picked her up and walked back to his room. He placed her on his bed and opened his second drawer and pulled out a small velvet pouch. He took out a beautiful platinum heart shaped pendant and tied it around her neck. "A precious gift for my precious love," he said and Violet gasped at the sheer beauty of it.

"Thank you, Lucas. I don't have anything so expensive to give you as a token of my love," she said.

"You have already given yourself to me baby. That's the most expensive gift ever," he said, kissing her forehead.

"You make me feel so happy," she gushed.

"I'm glad. So can you walk down.the aisle? He asked in concern

"Yes, I'm feeling much better now. " she said and he nodded happily.

"You're feeling better? Then get ready. We're going to get married, today," he announced, bringing her luggage from his walk-in closet. Violet rolled her eyes, she knew now his family would go crazy when he announced his plans to them.

Getting dressed, they left their room and climbed down the stairs. Lucas led her to the main building where everyone was sitting at a table for breakfast. They all looked up at them. Liam grinned and winked at her.

Her brothers grinned at her while attacking the delicious food in front of them. Lucas's mom smiled indulgently at both of them. "You both just on time. Join us for breakfast. It's so good to see Lucas normal again," she gushed, looking at them happily.

Serenity leaned towards her as she sat between her and Lucas. "Did the hungry lion let you sleep?" She chuckled at the blush that crept up Violet's neck and cheeks.

Lucas's dad smiled, "Good morning, both of you. So what are your plans for today?" He asked in a good mood.

"After breakfast, I'm getting married to Violet," said Lucas, attacking his scrambled eggs and toast. There was pin drop silence all around them as everyone gaped at him with rounded eyes.

"Can't you give us a week's time at least?" Asked his mom, her head, resting on her hand as she tried to persuade him to change his mind.

"Bro, seriously?" Asked Serenity, rolling her eyes.

"Yes, today. I've decided and I can't change my mind," said Lucas as everyone groaned out loud.

"Mom, how can I get a bridesmaid's dress at such notice?" Serenity wailed. Their mom looked at her with a look of utter horror on her face.

"Shouldn't we think of arranging a bridal dress for Violet first?" She asked Serenity. "What's the hurry son? Violet's with you. What difference will it make if you marry her next week? It will at least give us a little time to make arrangements."

"Mom you don't understand at all," he said, shaking his head. He wouldn't listen to anyone. He knew what he was doing.

"Then make me?" She asked her son. Lucas's dad looked at them with an amused expression on his face. So did Liam. The twins were only interested in their food.

"I just don't trust that Leilani. If she hears that I'm planning to marry Violet next week, she could plan anything to stop me from marrying her. So let me get married today, all of a sudden, then she can't do anything about it. I already would be married," he said and his dad nodded in understanding.

"It's his life, Eugene. Let him live in peace," said Lucas's dad, supporting him.

"Thanks dad," said Lucas.

"Ok fine. Then after breakfast we'll go to my friend Michelle's wedding boutique, "Dream Wedding Collection" nearby and buy whatever we need. Then we could get the Nevada marriage license and then arrange the wedding in our home," said Lucas's mom.

Everyone agreed and Lucas's mom spoke to her friend, Michelle on the phone and fixed an appointment with her. She spoke to the marriage officiant and fixed a time towards the afternoon. Satisfied they finished their breakfast.

"Sera, call aunt Estelle to come over and do our makeup," said Lucas's mom and Serenity picked up her phone and made the call. Aunt Estelle was their mom's sister who owned and ran a salon of her own. She was very innovative with her hairstyles and makeup and their mom trusted only her.

Violet stared at everything wide eyed. She didn't know anything about makeup and expensive clothes. "Violet, do you have any family to invite for your wedding?" Asked Lucas's dad, seeing her lost expression.

"No dad. My brothers are already here," she informed him.

"What about your parents?" Asked his mom.

"My mom and dad separated ten years ago. My mom brought us with her to my grandparents house. She was killed in a car accident last year," she informed quietly.

"I'm so sorry to hear that, dear," said Lucas's mom. She instantly felt bad for the young girl who might have been struggling with two younger siblings. Her big innocent eyes took in every conversation.

His mom felt a tug in her heart for the poor young girl. "I'm like your mom too. You can tell me anything you need. Ok?" She said and Violet nodded.

Violet liked Lucas's family very much. They were so unlike other billionaire families. She was glad that she met Lucas. He was a jewel, a treasure that God had sent for her. He had brought with him a silver lining to her otherwise dismal life. Now she was blissfully happy to be able to get married to him.

Chapter 21

Chapter Twenty-One

After breakfast Serenity was walking to her room, when Lucas called her. "Yes bro?" She asked.

"Thank you Sera. Thank you for bringing Violet to me. I can grant you whatever you want," he said, with a smile. Violet stood beside him with a smile on her face. She was thankful to Serenity for taking the pains and bringing her here to Lucas.

Serenity smiled with a a sadness in her eyes that she had always hidden from everyone's eyes. "You know what I want Lucas. I will always want it no matter how many years pass by. I might never be able to love again," she said and walked away.

"What does she want Lucas? Give her?" Said Violet.

Lucas nodded. "Yes, I think I've wronged her. She has always loved my best friend Alexander Dawson. Alexander has a notorious reputation and I didn't want Sera to fall for him and have her heart broken. We parted ways five years back after a vicious fight. We haven't contacted each other after that. But maybe I will, now. It's the only thing Sera wants from me," he said with a sigh.

The whole family went to the wedding store to get their dresses and tuxedos. Lucas's mom had called Tyler's family. Tyler's dad, Ethan Parker and his mom, Amanda Parker came along with Tyler's wife, River and sister Carmella.

After the brief introductions they all tried on different dresses and suits. After River cleared the misunderstanding between the two brothers, Tyler had called up and apologised to Lucas. They had patched up their differences and bonded just like before.

Lucas called his best friend, Alexander Dawson after five years of being away. He announced his wedding and asked about Alexander's whereabouts. Alexander was in San Francisco and could fly down to attend the wedding. The two friends apologised to each other and patched up. Feeling better, they made their purchases and to the marriage bureau to get their license. They all returned home and Lucas's mom made arrangements for the actual wedding ceremony and a dinner afterwards for the family and close friends.

The twins were too excited to get tuxedos. They ran around checking out the dinner menu, and the cocktail menu as well as the decor. Liam bonded well with them and they played together, stealing ice-creams in between.

Violet was whisked away to Serenity's room to get her ready much to Lucas's disappointment. "Why can't she get ready in my room, mom?" Protested Lucas.

"Give her a break, Lucas. Let her get ready in peace. You will get her after the ceremony. Won't you?" Said his mom, frustrated with his impatient attitude.

Lucas grumbled and walked off towards his room to sulk. Alexander called to inform that he had reached Las Vegas airport and he would pick up a black tuxedo for himself on the way, matching with Lucas's black tuxedo.

Violet was given a beauty bath and aunt Estelle had arrived with her attendants to get the bridal party ready. River, Carmella and Serenity were the bridesmaids with Serenity being the maid of honour. Lucas's mom and Tyler's mom looked into the preparations.

"Sera, Lucas has called Alexander today. He's on his way to attend our wedding, " informed Violet. Serenity's breath hitched and she looked at Violet with disbelief.

"He's coming?" She asked restlessly. Violet nodded at her. Serenity couldn't concentrate on anything after hearing the news of Alexander's visit. It had been five long years since she last saw him. She wondered what he did for a living now. Last time she saw him, he was at an illegal underground fight club, boxing with his bare knuckles for money.

Her parents loved him as a person but Lucas couldn't accept her feelings for Alexander. She never could confess her feelings to her parents out of fear of rejection. She sighed heavily and went about her task of getting Violet ready.

Violet's hair was done up in a romantically half updo with tendrils falling and framing her face. Her makeup was kept subtle and minimal. They fixed her ethereal off-shoulder lace trimmed dress with sheer long sleeves, a sheath silhouette, sweeping train with a high side slit. They fixed a lace trimmed veil to match and handed her a bouquet of red and white roses mixed with hydrangeas and ferns.

Violet wore he heart pendant that Lucas gave her. Lucas's mom came in to check the progress. She saw Violet and kissed her forehead.

"You're looking very beautiful, dear. Wear this, it belonged to Lucas's grandmother. She asked me to hand it to Lucas's wife before passing away. She loved Lucas dearly," said his mom, opening a box and taking out diamond teardrop earrings and fixing them to her ears. She took out a matching bracelet and fixed it to her wrist. "Now, you look complete."

"Thank you mom," said Violet and Lucas's mom patted her cheek and went away. The whole bridal party was ready and the marriage officiant would arrive in any minute.

"Are you ready? Take a deep breath," said River and Violet did as instructed to calm her jumpy nerves.

Eric Parker came into her room and smiled at her. "Let's go Violet. It's time. The officiant is here," he said escorting her out of the room. The bridal party followed her out.

Violet's heart thundered in her chest as she waited to he united with her Lucas forever. She was glad that God had at last granted her wish and she could have her happily ever after with the man of her dreams.

Serenity walked in a daze, looking all around her as if searching for someone. Violet knew that she was looking for her only love. Alexander Dawson.

Even after five years she still loved Alexander and Violet prayed that she too found her happiness with Alexander.

Epilogue

They went to the main building, where a small banquet hall was decorated with flowers and balloons. A wall was chosen to serve as the altar with sheer drapes and lavender floral decorations. The white decorations of the altar table against the lavender flowers made it stand out in contrast. Chairs were placed in front of the altar for the small number of guests invited at such short notice.

The officiant was already waiting there along with Lucas and a tall, handsome, muscular man. Violet's eyes met Lucas's as they stared at each other from across the banquet hall. He looked all the more handsome in his black tuxedo and white shirt. He had a red rose with a fern boutonniere.

The twins came with Liam and Tyler. They were the ring bearers, looking so smart and handsome in their black tuxedos. They came to hug her and she kissed their foreheads. Liam and Tyler were the groomsmen.

The moment Serenity walked into the room, she was agitated to see the man next to Lucas. From her behaviour, it was obvious to Violet who the man was. Alexander Dawson.

The bridal procession started with the twins leading and the brides-maids and the groomsmen following them to the music. At last, she took a deep breath and walked to the altar towards her groom escorted by Eric Parker.

He handed her to Lucas and the wedding ceremony started. Violet and Lucas stood through the ceremony and became one in the eyes of God. The lighting of the unity candle ceremony was over and the newlyweds posed for photographs. Serenity stuck to her and the twins to avoid all interaction with Alexander. She could feel his piercing gaze upon her wherever she went. It had been five years and she wasn't sure if he had any feelings for her. He never even loved her like she did. Maybe he was married. She didn't know. The dinner was delicious and everyone enjoyed themselves except Serenity.

Lucas pulled his wife to his body in a close dance. "Tonight's our wedding night. Are you ready for me?" He asked her, his eyes dark and dilated.

"Yes," she whispered.

"I've missed you so much," he confessed.

"Me too," she answered.

They danced together, lost in each other when Alexander pulled Serenity to himself for a dance.

"How long will you keep running from me?' He asked her, his hand holding her arm in a rough grip.

"You're hurting me Lex," she whispered, looking at his vice like grip on her.

She looked up at his sharp intake of breath. She forgot to breathe as she stared into his intense orbs. "Stay away from Logan Rush or I'll murder him, " he said, almost in a whisper.

She gaped at him wordlessly. Logan Rush was her colleague at Parker Suites who executed the interior designs that she advised. He was very professional and they shared a good work rapport. She didn't have any interest in him and neither did he. He was engaged to marry in a month.

Alexander left her and walked away abruptly towards his friend Lucas and his wife.

"Won't you introduce me to your lovely wife luke?" He asked.

Lucas grinned and wrapped an arm around Violet. "Meet my wife Violet. Violet this is my best friend, Alexander Dawson," he introduced.

"Hello Alexander, pleased to meet you," she said, shaking his hand.

"Enough," said Lucas, pulling her hand out of his hold.

"Possessive much?" Asked Alexander with a grin.

Lucas grinned too and they all talked for some more time. The wedding cake was cut. The speeches were over. The evening came to an end much to Lucas's satisfaction. Alexander sought out Serenity before leaving.

Lucas picked up Violet and escaped the party, carrying her to his bedroom, in his own building. He strode inside and locked his room. Depositing her on his bed, he climbed over her and stared at her with a lot of love and desire in his eyes.

"I love you, Violet, thanks for coming into my life," he whispered, caressing her soft cheeks.

"I love you too, Lucas," she replied back.

"Are you happy?" He asked.

"Very," she said and he claimed her lips. He was glad that she allowed him into her world, that she let him love her.

After ten days, they flew back to their beach in Santa Monica, LA with the twins. Life was complete and they couldn't ask for anything more. The twins started going to school and Violet concentrated on taking care of her family and starting her bakery.

Thus started their journey of true love and understanding, passion and endurance, happiness and faith in an eternal union that was destined for them. There's no greater gift of God than being able to unite with the one you love and be able to live with him forever and ever.

CPSIA information can be obtained
at www.ICGtesting.com
Printed in the USA
LVHW020403111122
732651LV00010B/904